ON COMMUNICATING

MARK H. McCORMACK

DOVE
BOOKS

Also available on audiocassette from Dove Audio

ISBN 0-7871-1269-0

Printed in the United States of America

Dove Books
8955 Beverly Boulevard
Los Angeles, CA 90048

Text design and layout by Frank Loose Design
Jacket design by Rick Penn-Kraus

First Printing: February 1998

10 9 8 7 6 5 4 3 2 1

Contents

No Grammar Lessons Here

L et me tell you what you won't find in this book. You won't find the complete rules of grammar and sentence composition.

You won't find a compendium of boilerplate letters that will tell you how to request a favor or deny someone credit or express condolences.

You won't find glossaries of the most frequently misused words and phrases in business writing.

You won't find references to esoteric rhetorical devices such as *anaphora*, which is the repetition of a word or phrase at the beginning of successive sentences for poetic effect (e.g., "You won't find . . .").

I also promise that this is the last time in these pages you will see phrases such as "subjunctive mood" and "restrictive clause."

And if you're looking to learn all about the principles of composition, tone, phrasing, and organization surrounding the written word, you've also come to the wrong place.

I'm not a professional grammarian or English teacher or professor of rhetoric or, for that matter, an amateur language maven. I have neither the credentials nor the burning interest to construe the subtleties of when to use "that" rather than "which" or "whom" rather than "who."

I'm also not a pedant. If someone misuses a word or misplaces a preposition, I don't feel the urge to correct that person. I remember the last time someone did that to me. I also remember that I didn't enjoy it much.

I also know that there are good books out there that already cover the subject well. If I wanted to toss my hat into that crowded ring, I would have called this book *McCormack on Writing*.

But I didn't. Instead it's called *On Communicating*, and there's a reason.

For one thing, the spoken word, whether it takes the form of a speech, a roundtable discussion, a phone call, or an intimate one-on-one conversation, is a far more prevalent form of communication than the written word. We talk more than we write. And we probably accomplish more through talking than we do through writing. If the spoken and written word comprise the two categories of communicating, it seems absurd to limit this book to what is clearly the less dominant category and ignore what is clearly the more important form of communication.

When I think about what people expect to get out of any form of communication, the list of basic goals can get lengthy. People communicate:

- to report

- to persuade

- to establish rapport

- to sell

- to win

- to criticize

- to correct

- to instruct

- to elevate themselves

- to defeat or humiliate the other side

- to record history

- to set a deal down in writing

- to get attention (or respect or honor. . .)

I could go on. My point is, using "whom" rather than "who" correctly won't necessarily help you achieve any of these goals. I know I've never been persuaded, charmed, or impressed simply because someone's grammar and syntax were perfect.

Like the rest of the world, I'm more interested in what people have to say, how they present themselves vocally and physically, whether they seek out or avoid eye contact with me, whether they let me speak my piece or interrupt, and whether they're actually listening to me or are mentally rehearsing their comeback lines. I'm looking for those moments when they suddenly become animated or when their body language doesn't quite mesh with the words they're saying.

In my mind, these (and many more) are the true elements of effective communication. If you can understand and control them, you can achieve the goals cited above—and it won't matter whether you use "whom" or "who" correctly.

I feel obliged to mention all this at the beginning. It's my attempt at truth in advertising. It's also my official warning to readers: If you think improving as a communicator is a matter of mastering the various forms of communication, then you are in for a rude surprise. Appearance and format and adherence to quaint rules and traditions do not make the message (although they *do* make the message easier to digest).

In this book, I will try to get readers to think more clearly not only about the substance of their communications, but about all the forces floating around in the workplace that affect communication.

For example, in chapter 9, I won't tell you how to write the perfect résumé: how to set it up on the page; how to organize it from most recent employment to last; or how to keep it to a single page. Instead, I'll tell you why you should evaluate what the résumé doesn't say about you. In other words, what's the résumé in your mind rather than on the page? Then I'll tell you why your cover letter is even more important than the résumé itself (a hint: all résumés look and sound alike; the cover letter is where you can shine, where you reveal the real you). I'll even discuss the biggest mystery of all: What happens to your letter after it leaves your desk.

At this point, you should be asking who I am to teach and preach on communicating.

I've already told you that I'm not an English instructor. In fact, I'm a lawyer by training, which, if you've ever read a legal brief, is hardly the most promising spawning ground for clear, concise communication.

My main credential is that I run a sports marketing company, which I started thirty-six years ago in Cleveland, Ohio, with $500 in capital, called International Management Group, or simply IMG.

We represent hundreds of well-known athletes such as Arnold Palmer (my first client), Tiger Woods, Joe Montana, Chris Webber, Annika Sorenstam, Monica Seles, and Andre Agassi. In recent years, we have branched out into the representation of classical musicians and singers such as Itzhak Perlman, James Galway, and Dawn Upshaw.

We create and manage events, everything from the Toyota World Match Play at Wentworth to a José Carreras concert in Singapore to the Detroit Grand Prix motor race to "Jesus Christ Superstar" in Sydney, Australia to the Dubai Snooker Classic.

We represent the Nobel Foundation. We have helped develop the commercial interests of Wimbledon and the Royal and Ancient Golf Club of St. Andrews.

Our television arm, Trans World International, has represented the international broadcast rights for sports properties such as the Olympic Games, the World and European Figure Skating championships, the National Football League, all the major golf and tennis championships, and the twenty-four hours of Le Mans. It is also the world's largest independent producer of television sports programming.

Today, IMG has two thousand employees generating over a billion dollars in revenue out of seventy-one offices in twenty-nine countries around the world. In the interval between my handshake agreement with Arnold Palmer (which helped me start the company) and now, I think I've faced every conceivable communication problem a manager and human being can face.

My other credential is that I have written books.

In 1984, I wrote *What They Don't Teach You at Harvard Business School*, which sold well enough (actually, it was a number one bestseller for months) to persuade publishers to let me write a second book, *The Terrible Truth About Lawyers*. Since then, I've continued writing business books (this is my ninth). I also write a monthly newsletter, "Success Secrets," and a weekly management column that is syndicated to newspapers and magazines around the world. I give speeches on management and career issues as well as on the business of sports to corporations, trade associations, business conferences, and universities. So you see, when I'm not running our company, I spend a considerable portion of my time not only thinking about communicating but actually doing it.

As a result, the communicating examples you'll read here are personal. In almost every case, they involved me or our company. In other words, they're real. In some cases, I look brilliant. In others, not so brilliant. I cite the triumphs and disasters with equal liberality so that you can emulate the former and do not repeat the latter.

My only caveat (as I have said of the three previous volumes in this series, *On Negotiating*, *On Selling*, and *On Managing*) is that this communicating primer has a beginning, middle, and end. I've sometimes described my earlier books as "popcorn." Like a bag of popcorn, you can dip in anywhere and find a morsel to chew on. This book is different. It begins with the basic communicating tools that everyone must master and leads you steadily to increasingly more complicated situations and advanced techniques. It's meant to be read from start to finish.

With that in mind, let's get started.

CHAPTER 1

How Anyone Can Communicate with Me

I like to think I'm a bit of an iconoclast in most of my business affairs. Whether I'm selling, negotiating, managing people and clients, competing against other companies, or organizing my time, I try to not be a slave to conventional wisdom. I like to push the envelope and stir things up.

However, if there's a business discipline where I am a true traditionalist, it has to be in the area of communicating—because the essence of communicating never changes. The goals remain the same: to introduce, instruct, persuade, or assert authority. Although the tools we use to achieve these goals may change—from yesterday's handwritten notes to today's E-mail—the architecture of effective communication remains the same:

- Know your subject.

- Know your audience.

- Know your medium.

- Given the choice, be brief rather than wordy.

- Keep in mind the difference between a forceful and a belligerent tone.

- Trust the power of a carefully chosen word.

- Never forget how you would like people to communicate with you.

This last point is surely the most important. Reduced to its essence, it's a variation on the Golden Rule: Communicate with others as you would have them communicate with you.

All of us know this in our bones. We've heard it all our lives. When we misspoke as children, our parents would chide us: "That's no way to talk. How would you like it if someone said that to you?"

It's no different as adults in business. Before you can learn how to communicate properly, you must calculate how you want the rest of the world to communicate with you. Here are my preferences.

1. TALK UP, NOT DOWN, TO ME.

People have two choices at the start of any communication. They can assume their audience is knowledgeable about the subject at hand and tailor their remarks accordingly. They don't overexplain. They don't condescend. They don't omit crucial details because "they're too complicated."

Or they can assume their audience knows nothing. As a result, they "dumb down" their remarks.

Either approach is legitimate depending on the circumstances. What bothers me, though, is when people assume the know-nothing approach without checking with me first.

When I communicate with people—in person, on the phone, or in writing—I always give them the benefit of the doubt. I assume they know as much as I do. At the start of a relationship, I prefer people to extend the same courtesy to me. I want them to talk up to me, not down. I want them to assume that I'm a quick study. When the discussion sails over my head, I'll let them know that I'm falling behind. I don't have a problem saying, "I have no idea what you're talking about."

People don't like to be lectured at or treated like dummies. So if you want to communicate with me, assume the best, not the worst.

2. SURPRISE ME.

I am the recipient (or is it victim?) of so much routine communication—memos, sales pitches, junk mail, etc.—that when someone approaches me with anything remotely out of the ordinary, I pay attention.

For example, at 5:30 A.M. on March 11, 1995, I was reading the newspaper and having a cup of coffee in my room at the Peninsula Hotel in Los Angeles when I got a phone call from a young Australian named James Pardoe. The conversation went something like this:

Pardoe: "Mr. McCormack, I know you get up at 4:30 every morning and I would really like to work for you. I thought maybe you could have a cup of coffee or tea with me."

Me: "Where are you?"

Pardoe: "I am down in the lobby."

Me: "How did you know I was here?"

Pardoe: "I knew you stayed at the Peninsula and I have been calling the hotel waiting until you came into town."

Me: "Where did you come from?"

Pardoe: "I live in Malibu but because the highways were flooded, I had to get up at three o'clock this morning to drive in."

Me: "Well, I can see you in sixty minutes in the lobby."

If he had called at a normal hour, I probably wouldn't have agreed to see him on such short notice. But he employed the element of surprise. That always works with me.

3. Tempt me.

As I've said, I'm slightly jaded. After thirty-five years in business, I often think I've seen everything before. But I'm still a sucker for any form of communication that means more money for our company or me. (Heck, I still tear open the Publishers Clearing House envelope, convinced that I have just won $10 million!)

If you can lace your letter or phone call with even the slightest suggestion that we can make money together, you are communicating effectively with me.

4. FLATTER ME.

I'm human. When I get letters from strangers telling me they enjoyed a speech I gave or how my "Harvard" book changed their life, I keep reading. Don't kid yourself. You would too.

That's the power of carefully calibrated, mildly exaggerated flattery. A stroke of the ego will always capture attention.

But don't go overboard, don't make silly errors, and don't be insincere. If someone writes that my book changed his or her life but misspells my name, I might naturally question the impact I've had on that person's life. I would also stop reading.

5. TELL ME WHAT YOU WANT.

It never ceases to amaze me how people can write the most lucid and eloquent letters to me and yet neglect the most important point: They don't tell me what they want.

This happens most often with letters from people introducing themselves to our company. They tell me who they are and what they have achieved. They often go so far as to tell me how they can help our company. But by letter's end, when I'm favorably impressed by their credentials and presumably most receptive to any request they have in mind, I'm left staring at the piece of paper wondering, "What do they want me to do? Do they want to meet with me? Do they expect a written reply? Do they want me to pass their letters on to the appropriate executive at our company?"

I try to respond in some way to every letter that comes into my office. But if you want me to do something for you, don't make me guess. Tell me.

6. TELL ME I'M WRONG.

I've run my own business for most of my adult life. One of the natural consequences of being the boss is that few people have the courage or confidence to disagree with me, and fewer still will tell me I'm wrong. It's the "Emperor's Clothes" syndrome; it afflicts all bosses, whether they have 3 employees or 300,000.

But disagreement and bare-knuckled criticism of my opinions are precisely the kinds of messages I need to be hearing every day. So when someone inside or outside the company takes a strong position and tells me I'm wrong, I pay attention.

I have no illusions that I'm infallible. But like everyone else, I have a problem figuring out *when* my fallibility is on display. If you can pinpoint those occasions, you're not insulting me, you're doing me a big favor. You're communicating with me in a way that most people refuse to do—and I'm grateful.

The Tools at Your Disposal

The Illusion of Communication

When she heard I was writing a book on communicating, a good friend insisted I include the following quote: "The problem with communication is the illusion it has been achieved."

She has a point.

There are at least two parties in any form of communication: one to send the message and one to receive it. Unfortunately, it's rare that both parties are on the same wavelength, that one side is hearing what the other side is actually saying.

There's a good reason for this. In the interval between the sending and receiving of any communication, a lot of distracting forces come into play that either distort the message or warp our ability to interpret it properly. Here are some of the more pernicious forces in the workplace that create the illusion of communication.

1. FAILING TO CONFIRM THE MESSAGE.

I often think that military communication is the ideal by which all other forms of business communication should be judged. In the heat of battle, military personnel talking to each other via less-than-one hundred percent-reliable electronic devices must constantly confirm that they've received a message *and* that they understand it. When lives are at stake, the military recognizes that communication signals can break up or get jammed. Nothing is taken for granted. Every message must be confirmed.

It's not a particularly poetic or lyrical way to communicate, and it is time consuming. But it accomplishes something many people in business overlook. It establishes that the message is coming through—loud and clear.

Too many executives operate under the illusion that there is a perfect correlation between what they say in the workplace and what their subordinates hear. If they make a request or give an order, they often assume that their subordinates comprehend it perfectly. They never bother to seek immediate confirmation that the message has gotten through.

To these executives I would recommend the following military exercise. The next time you ask subordinates or colleagues to do something for you, don't let them leave the room without also asking, "Could you play that back for me?" You might be surprised at how garbled and distorted their responses are. Given the high percentage of foul-ups and misunderstandings in the workplace, you shouldn't be.

2. FORGETTING THE CALL TO ACTION.

In early 1996, I returned from an amazing business conference where I had met at least thirty decisionmakers who wanted to do business with our company. Knowing that it was easy to be overwhelmed by so many new contacts and that it was physically impossible for me to respond to each one personally in a timely manner—and also knowing how easy it was to push these new contacts to the side and move on to other pressing matters once I returned home—I decided to gather my thoughts in a lengthy memo about the conference. I described each person I met, providing everything from my personal impressions of them to their job title and corporate addresses. I also outlined the areas of our company they were interested in.

Then I did something I've never tried before. I included a paragraph called "Desired Action," set off in bold type at the end of each contact entry. In it I designated which of our company representatives I wanted to follow up with these important individuals. I outlined how I expected this follow-up to proceed and what subjects might be discussed. Lastly, I set specific deadlines for everyone to get back to me with their results.

I mention this not only because it was something new for me but because it attacks a major flaw in most business communications. If failing to confirm that your message has gotten through is the biggest communication illusion, then fail-ing *to ask for a specific action* is a close second.

You know this is true if you've read as many documents as I have that state facts and opinions but, in the end, never tell me what I'm supposed to do with all this information.

It doesn't matter what form of communication you pre-fer—whether it's memos, letters, phone calls, speeches, or E-mail—if you're not clearly stating a desired action by the end of it, you're not really communicating. Your memo, letter, phone call, or E-mail is an illusion.

3. FEARING TO DISAGREE.

Have you ever been in a meeting where the boss says some-thing that is patently false or renders a verdict that is based on flawed information? And no one speaks up to disagree?

That silence is another illusion of communication. It's called the Disagreement Fallacy. Just because people don't disagree with you doesn't automatically mean they agree.

As a boss myself, I'm well aware that it takes courage for some people to tell me I'm wrong. In fact, as a manager, my sin-gle biggest worry is that people are not telling me the truth—because the truth is what I most desperately need.

I want to be challenged. I want to hear disagreement. As a result, I'm very wary when I don't hear it. I have no illu-sions that silence means people are in complete agreement with me. Actually, it only means I have a lot more commu-nicating to do.

I suggest all bosses treat the roaring silence from their colleagues with the same skepticism.

4. IGNORING THE BEAUTY OF ARGUMENTS.

The corollary to the Disagreement Fallacy is this: Just because someone argues with your position, it doesn't necessarily mean they disagree with you or are against you.

I wonder how many misunderstandings and irreparably damaged relationships have been born in the workplace because someone strenuously argued a point of business with someone else.

One of the great satisfactions of conducting meetings at our company is that our senior managers can freely disagree with one another in such a public forum—and it doesn't affect their relationships. These are people who have worked together for twenty or more years. They're concerned about each other outside the office. They stay at each other's homes (rather than use a hotel) when they visit each other's cities. They take vacations together. That sort of camaraderie is admirable on many fronts, but it really pays off in effective communication.

The arguments in our meetings can be loud, vehement, and sometimes comically nasty. But it doesn't mean that people don't respect each other or won't get together for dinner later that day. In my mind, that argumentative openness is close to ideal.

If you don't have it in your organization's meetings, you're probably not communicating well at all.

5. CHOOSING THE WRONG MEDIUM.

Sometimes the biggest flaw for our communications is the medium we choose.

For example, we have an executive in a distant part of the globe who is notorious for never responding to memos or faxes. But he is religious about returning phone calls. The telephone is his preferred medium of communication. Thus, writing to him will give you only an illusion that you are communicating with him. Calling him will give you the real thing.

Likewise, I know another executive who is slightly dyslexic. He has trouble digesting lengthy written communications. But he's a brilliant individual and has compensated for this deficiency by developing virtually perfect recall of everything he hears. Thus, if I want to communicate with him, I talk to him. If I write to him, I know only a fraction of my message will get through and I can't be sure which fraction that will be.

I suspect all of our messages would break through more clearly if we gave a little thought to how our intended targets receive them.

ELEVEN INSTRUCTIONS THAT MEAN NOTHING

I met a screenwriter not long ago in a social situation. I told him I admired his work and then expressed some empathy for how hard his job must be.

I said, "I imagine the worst part must be being locked up in a room by yourself all day and having to create dialogue that sounds natural out of thin air."

He immediately corrected me. "Writing in a room is the fun part," he said. "The worst part is that your work is judged and critiqued by people who have no idea how to improve what they're criticizing. If they don't like a script, they say something like, 'Can you make it more dramatic,' or 'It needs more edge.'—as if that insight is going to light some thousand-watt bulb over my head. I guess that's what really bothers me the most. Their so-called instructions mean nothing."

The screenwriter's remarks hit home with me, because, frankly, I think all of us are guilty of handing out instructions that don't really instruct. We think we're delivering a message with the glib or pointed comments we make to our associates, but we probably overestimate how much of the message really gets through. Consider the following so-called instructions that all of us hear or employ during the course of a business day:

1. "This proposal needs more focus."

2. "Make it go away."

3. "We have to sell more."

4. "Just do it."

5. "Get a better handle on this."

6. "This needs more work."

7. "Figure it out and get back to me."

8. "Make lots of money for us from this."

9. "See what this fellow wants."

10. "Breathe some life into this project."

11. "I'm not convinced. Convince me."

These comments remind me of the scene in the movie *Amadeus* where the Emperor of Austria goes backstage to congratulate Mozart after the premiere of his operatic masterpiece, *The Marriage of Figaro*. The Emperor tells Mozart the opera was marvelous but the music made too many demands on his royal ear. "There were too many notes," he says.

Mozart demurs that he used only as many notes as the piece required, no more, no less.

The Emperor persists with his "too many notes" critique and fatuously suggests that the opera would improve if Mozart took out some notes.

Mozart caustically asks, "Which notes should I remove, your majesty?"

An instruction isn't really doing its job if it confuses or angers or otherwise fails to motivate the person receiving the instruction.

The flaw in all of the instructions above is that they lack one or more of the essential elements of an effective instruction. An effective instruction contains the following components.

1. It explains why you want something done.

A good instruction is like a mission statement. It defines a specific goal and the reason the goal is worth pursuing. If you give someone directions to your office (one of the most common forms of instruction), the goal or mission is usually implied: You want to meet that person face to face. But there are many everyday instructions where the why is not implied or obvious and needs to be explicitly stated.

For example, let's say I tell someone, "Breathe some life into this proposal." Other than suggesting that I'm not impressed with the material, that's not a very clear instruction. It's so vague it might not even generate any immediate action. But if I preface it by saying, "This proposal is the most important document we will be sending all year to our most important customer," that adds some urgency to my request. If nothing else, I've reordered the instructee's priorities and given him a reason to obey my instruction.

2. IT DEFINES AN END RESULT.

A good instruction not only gets people started, it tells them when to stop. Telling someone, "This report needs more work," is a dangerously vague instruction because it doesn't explain how much more work is required. Theoretically, the instructee can work on it forever. A better instruction would add, "When you get accurate projections and get Bob and Ted to sign off on it, show it to me again."

3. IT EXPLAINS SPECIFICALLY HOW YOU WANT THE TASK DONE.

A good instruction usually comes with a manual of proper techniques and procedures. I suppose there are people at our company who would know exactly what I meant if I said, "Take care of this" or "Make this go away." They've worked with me long enough to know the procedures I would follow.

But the majority of people would require a step-by-step procedural to really do the job right. Thus, when I ask an associate to call an executive I know at another company, I'll tell the associate when to call, what to say to the executive's assistant to make sure they get through, and possibly which topics I want discussed and which ones to avoid. It's amazing how many managers forget or don't take the time to include these technical details in their instructions. If you tell people what to do but not how to do it, don't be surprised when they don't follow through in the way you wanted.

4. IT PROVIDES A TIME FRAME.

A good instruction comes with a deadline. "I need this" is not as good as "I need this right away." "I need this right away," in turn, is not as good as "I need this by 5 P.M. tomorrow." The best instructions are very specific about the clock.

5. IT DEFINES SUCCESS AND FAILURE.

A good instruction lets you know when you've gone too far and when you haven't gone far enough. In terms of giving directions to your house, it's like saying, "If you pass a red church on the right you've gone one block past our house." In business, it means defining what's acceptable or unacceptable to you.

The problem with telling people, "Let's make a lot of money on this deal," is that it begs the question: What constitutes "a lot of money"? How much is enough? If you don't tell your people that you expect at least $50,000 from a certain transaction, you have only yourself to blame when they come back satisfied with $25,000.

I'm sure some people in our company think that I'm too detailed, too controlling, maybe even too long-winded with some of the instructions I've given out over the years. But that's usually what it takes to make sure my instructions mean something rather than nothing.

ALL HEADLINE, NO TEXT

Have you ever been seduced into buying a tabloid newspaper or supermarket magazine on the spur of a moment because of a lurid or sensational headline? Then, when you turn to the inside page, you realize you've been suckered—that there are no facts and no story behind the headline, only conjecture and malicious speculation.

If this happens to you three or four more times, you might stop buying that publication—because it has no credibility.

The same thing happens with people.

I can't count the number of times someone has come into my office and impressed me with a wonderful idea that will make our company a lot of money. And then days, weeks, months go by and I never hear anything else about the idea. In my mind, people who behave this way are the equivalent of the sensationalist tabloids: all headline, no text.

If they do this regularly with me or their colleagues, they risk losing much of their credibility.

One reason this is so common in business, I suppose, can be blamed on the natural division between thinkers and doers that exists in every organization.

No matter where you work, you will always find that a certain percentage of your employees are classic "idea people." They love to dream and speculate and fantasize. Because of their training or personality, they can transform seemingly disparate sets of facts into bold new concepts that can sustain a company's growth for years.

Likewise, every organization needs a healthy percentage of people who are classic "executors." They're not particularly creative, but once you point them in the right direction, they have the tenacity, endurance, and attention to detail that guarantees they will finish whatever they start.

The big successes in corporate life, however, are the people who manage to do both. They not only have the talent to come up with ideas, but they have the fortitude to make these ideas come to life.

Unfortunately, if you are not already an idea person, I don't have any magic wand that will suddenly make you creative. However, if you are a creative type and find that your brilliant ideas are regularly missing the mark or falling short of your expectations, here are four points that could protect or restore your credibility and help you avoid the tag "All Headline, No Text."

1. BE PATIENT WITH IDEAS.

I've often thought that patience is the most important quality for nurturing ideas. The distance between *idea* and *result* is usually a lengthy process. It doesn't happen overnight. A lot of creative people have trouble accepting that. They want instant results, instant gratification, and instant acclaim for their concepts. When these instant results don't materialize, they get frustrated, abandon the idea, and move on to something else. That's why so many good concepts are orphaned near birth—because their parents didn't have the patience to wait for them to grow.

2. KNOW YOUR TIMETABLE.

The first step for developing more patience (or at least reducing your impatience) is to create a realistic timetable for making your idea happen. The timetable could be two weeks or two years, but if you have a realistic notion of the time required to nurture an idea, you are less likely to give up on the concept.

I remember a few years ago when we came up with the idea for a world golf ranking. I knew it could take at least three years to get the concept up and running: to perfect it, accredit it, fund it, promote it, and distribute it. That three-year period was the timetable inside my head—and it sustained me through the many setbacks we encountered in bringing the idea to life.

3. BROADCAST YOUR TIMETABLE.

Once you establish a timetable, it's usually a good idea to share that information with your superiors. The worst thing you can do is to get your bosses excited about an idea and have them expecting it signed, sealed, and delivered in four weeks when you know it will more likely require six months.

There's no virtue in being patient yourself if you haven't conditioned your superiors to be patient as well.

4. Update, update, update.

The easiest way to sabotage your credibility and your idea is to assume that your bosses know how hard you're working on it. The truth is, they probably don't. That's why you have to provide them with regular updates on how your concept is progressing.

As a boss myself, with only a glancing awareness of some of the dozens of ideas our people are working on, it's only natural for me to assume that the people who consistently update me on their projects are the people who are working the hardest on them—and that those who don't update me are not working that hard. It might not be fair, but what other evidence does a boss have to rely on?

Keep that in mind as you develop your next brilliant idea. Once you've intrigued people with your exciting headline, doesn't it make sense to let them know that you've started working on the text?

The Danger of the Half-Baked Idea

One of our New York executives was heading out the door the other day for a meeting with one of our most significant licensing clients when a colleague grabbed him and said, "I have this great idea for your client, which you might want to bring up at your meeting."

As the colleague explained his idea with increasing enthusiasm and urgency, the licensing executive interrupted him.

"Look," he said, "if you think I'm going to my client with this half-baked idea, you're crazy. You and I know how ideas pop up and how sometimes they work out and sometimes they fall apart. But my client doesn't. He likes everything gift wrapped in a box with a ribbon around it. If I mention this project to him, and for some reason it doesn't happen, then I look foolish."

Our licensing executive was making an important point. The danger of the half-baked idea is not that it might never see the light of day, but that bringing it up and failing to make it happen can chip away at your credibility.

When I first started out, I realized that there were two ways I could present an idea to a client. One way was to literally tell the client everything I was working on. If there were ten projects, all unresolved but in various stages of development, I would go through them and get the client's opinion on each.

The second way was to play it close to the vest. I wouldn't mention a project until I was 100 percent sure it was real. Only then would I present it for the client's approval.

I soon realized that each approach represented its own set of risks and rewards.

On the one hand, if I held off presenting an idea until it was a sure thing, there could conceivably be long periods of time when I wasn't interacting with the client. The client would be left with the impression that I wasn't working very hard for him.

On the other hand, if I ran to the client with every idea that popped into my head, I also ran the risk of damaging my credibility. If none of the ten projects on my plate worked out, I wouldn't blame the client for wondering about my competence.

Which route you choose to present your ideas (and either approach is fine) depends upon whom you are dealing with. Some people can handle a wide assortment of ideas and can accept the fact that most, if not all, of them will fall through the cracks. Other people can't be bothered with your half-baked ideas; they want them signed, sealed, and delivered.

For example, in my early years with Arnold Palmer, I slowly learned that telling him about all the projects I was working on was only muddying the waters—because Arnold would start thinking about them. And thinking about them took his mind off his golf game.

For example, if I happened to mention that the Peruvian golf association wanted him to play in the Peruvian Open, he would regularly ask me, "What's going on with the Peruvian deal? Am I going to Peru?"

I eventually realized that it was best for all concerned not to bring it up. First, I would determine if Arnold was free the week of the Peruvian Open. Then I would encourage the Peruvians to find a sponsor for Arnold's visit and wait until we had a firm deal to mention it to Arnold. In the meantime, I protected that date on Arnold's calendar. If he made other plans, that's when I would be forced to disclose the invitation from Peru. Until then, though, I would play it close to the vest.

THE ART OF EXPLANATION

I've always been intrigued by the fact that a lot of top athletes, who are very good at their particular sport, have very little insight into how they excel at what they do. They are incapable of breaking down their technique and explaining it to a novice.

This isn't too surprising. Much of what an athlete does relies heavily on instinct, touch, and grace. These attributes are hard to codify and explain.

For example, I've never seen a golfer who could hook a golf ball better than Arnold Palmer. But if you asked Arnold how to hook a shot (that is, intentionally drive the ball to the right of the target and then bend it back to the left), he'd probably say, "You just hook it." He'd grab a club and, largely by feeling it, hook the ball. The fact that he's the best at doing it doesn't guarantee that he's the best at explaining it.

On the other side of the spectrum, you have golf instructors who are horrible at hooking the ball, but who can deconstruct every element of your swing and rebuild it so that you can hook the ball. They will outline the aerodynamic principles involved when the club head sweeps across the ball and imparts a spin that makes the ball go right to left. They'll use vivid imagery and analogies to make their point and they'll repeat the lessons until you learn. (To be fair, I'm sure Arnold Palmer knows the technical elements behind a hook; I just don't think he has the patience to explain it six times while he waits for someone to get it.) The fact that they are not the best at doing it doesn't mean they aren't the best at explaining it.

In sports, those who can, do. Those who can't, teach.

Business executives don't have that luxury. They're expected to do it *and* explain it well. If they are superstars at selling or negotiating or cost-cutting, they can strengthen the company by imparting that wisdom to their subordinates. Unfortunately, not enough executives take the art of explanation seriously. They're too busy doing to make time for explaining.

I don't buy this. I learned a long time ago that taking the five minutes to explain a task correctly would ultimately save me five hundred minutes of doing it myself or reexplaining. As a wise man said, "If you give a man a fish, he eats for a day. If you teach a man to fish, he eats for the rest of his life."

When it comes to explanations, I'm proactive rather than reactive. I don't wait for people to ask me, "How do you sign a client?" or "How do you handle a meddlesome parent?" By then it might be too late (presumably they're asking because they're having trouble in those areas). I offer explanations before some of our people even realize they need it.

In fact, my first book, *What They Don't Teach You at Harvard Business School*, grew out of a series of lectures I used to give to our people in the 1970s. We were a small, growing company in a field where we were basically writing the rules as we went along. I wanted our people to know how we did things, so I would periodically gather everyone in a room and deliver a mini-lecture on everything from "the best time to renegotiate a contract" to "writing deal memos that our lawyers can understand."

(Old habits die hard. In recent years, we have regularly gathered several dozen of our younger executives in Cleveland, Ohio, for a three-day refresher course on client management. Our thinking is that someone in London managing a young violin prodigy can learn from someone in Cleveland managing a tennis prodigy—and vice versa. Plus, explaining our company's heritage to new employees has some value.

No one asked for the course. But I realized we needed it when I noticed that many of our newer people didn't appreciate aspects of client management that I had always taken for granted. The first rule of explanation is: The more self-evident a concept or procedure is, the greater the need for explaining it to others.)

In every situation there is the risk that the subject is being underexplained or overexplained—because the explainer is concentrating too much on the subject rather than the audience.

I see this in our company. We have one executive who talks to me the same way he talks to a twenty-two-year-old fresh out of college. If he's explaining a sports concept he'll describe it from every angle and add a dozen fascinating digressions from his encyclopedic knowledge of sports. Now, that broad history lesson might be worthwhile to a newcomer at our company, but it's overkill with me. Yet he's so focused on the subject (and perhaps the sound of his voice) that he forgets I don't need a class in Sports Marketing 101. He could speak in shorthand with me and be more effective.

To explain well, you have to pay as much attention to the intelligence and experience of the person who needs the explanation as you do to the subject you are explaining. You have to explain in a way that recognizes all the elements that your audience doesn't need to know. With some people I only have to make one point to give a proper explanation. With others I might have to make eight points to get the message across.

For example, before a sales call, I could tell most of our senior executives, "Be sure to let the other side name the number first," and they would know exactly what I mean. They've heard this litany before.

If I gave the same instruction to a younger executive, he or she would probably accept my authority and carry it out. But the instruction would be pointless if I didn't elaborate, justify it by citing examples where the technique had worked previously, and provide step-by-step instructions for making it work.

If there is an art to explanation the artistry is in knowing who you're talking to. If you know your audience, you'll know which details are essential and which are extraneous.

I was given a blunt reminder of this the first time I met the King of Sweden. It was at a dinner at someone's home in Stockholm. The invitation said 6:30 P.M. As 6:30 approached I became involved in a phone conversation in my hotel room. Figuring that these affairs start off slowly with drinks, I wasn't too concerned about being late. I arrived a few minutes before seven o'clock—and committed a major *faux pas*. The King was already there. The protocol is: No one arrives after the King!

But no one had explained that to me. Perhaps they assumed that I frequently dine with royalty. But this was my first King. I'm told the King still jokes about it. But someone should have told me, "Don't be late for this dinner."

How to Benchmark with a Human Touch

I began this book promising that you wouldn't hear any buzzwords. But of all the management buzzwords floating out there in the corporate ether, my favorite is "benchmarking." If you haven't heard the phrase before, it is an old Bell Telephone innovation whereby an organization identifies the best products and methods in its field and then compares its own performance against these "benchmarks." It's a three-step process. First, you identify the best in your field. Then you tear it apart to see what makes it the best. Finally, you adjust your performance standards to duplicate this benchmark.

Automobile companies are big on benchmarking. If General Motors engineers regard Toyota cars as the best in their class, they'll buy a Toyota and strip it down to see what Toyota is doing that GM should be doing. They'll list all of the Toyota innovations that impress them and figure out how they can reach the same quality level in GM cars.

It's easy to see why benchmarking is so appealing. How can you dislike a concept that forces organizations to continually raise their standards?

Where benchmarking becomes a little problematic is when you apply it to people. It's one thing to strip down a mechanical device, whether it's a car or a calculator, to see what makes it work. It's a little more difficult with human beings. You can't simply tear down your top performers, analyze their most valuable qualities, and then graft those features onto the rest of your workforce.

35

Benchmarking with talented professionals requires an approach that's a great deal more subtle than an engineer holding a screwdriver and clipboard.

The first hurdle is getting talented people to admit that someone else may be doing a better job than they are. If you're building cars, it's easy to tell whether or not your cars are the benchmark in a given category. Your gas mileage is there for everyone to see in the EPA numbers. Even a cursory examination of a car's fit and finish—running your fingers over the paint job, opening and shutting the car doors—will tell you if your car has room to improve.

It's trickier with people. People don't usually respond in a positive manner when you hold up your top salesperson or most popular manager and command the staff, "Be like them!" People's egos get in the way. They're as loathe to admit their faults as they are to admit other people's successes. They also don't appreciate the implied criticism in your command.

But people do respond to praise, and they crave praise when it is showered on someone else.

My friend Gordon Forbes, a successful South African entrepreneur who founded the largest lighting manufacturer in the southern hemisphere, once described how he liked to walk through the facility when he was setting up his lighting factory.

At first, whenever Forbes came across an employee who was doing something wrong—e.g., constructing a light bulb incorrectly—his automatic reaction was to get mad at the employee and berate him. "How can you put that filament together that way? It should be done like this." And then he would demonstrate how to do it properly. Showing people how you want things done is good management.

But Forbes soon realized that he was basically criticizing his employees in front of their coworkers. Instead of looking for mistakes on his factory tours, he started looking for examples of excellence. As Forbes puts it, "Don't find the worst at your company and criticize it. Find the best at your company and praise it."

That's the essence of benchmarking with people. And it appears in many guises in an organization.

A few years ago the head of our Hamburg office concocted an "extraordinary" deal with a German hotel to distribute my monthly newsletter, *Success Secrets*, to its most valued guests. In the grand scheme of things, the money involved was minuscule (less than I could earn giving a thirty-minute speech). But it was extraordinary nevertheless because it showed flair and initiative. More important, the concept could be duplicated with hotels in at least fifty other cities where we have offices—at which point the accumulated revenues would not be minuscule. Our man in Hamburg had created a new revenue stream.

There was more than one way to disclose this "benchmark" to other executives. I could have sent a memo to the heads of our various offices saying "Look what our man in Hamburg did. Why don't you do it too?" I could have suggested the idea without making any reference to Hamburg.

In the end I heeded Gordon Forbes and settled for mere praise. I sent our Hamburg chief a congratulatory letter for being a "super salesman." Of course, I made sure every office chief around the world received a copy of this document.

That's the beauty of benchmarking with praise. You don't always have to badger or bully employees to raise their performance standards. Praise the individuals who are setting those high standards and the message will come through loud and clear to everyone else within earshot.

A GOOD CRITIC THINKS TWICE BEFORE GOING PUBLIC

In my previous book, *On Managing*, I devoted a lot of pages to the tremendous benefits of praising people in public. A good executive should not shy away from saying the same good things about an associate in public that he says in private. If you praise a subordinate in front of his peers, you not only paint yourself as a generous boss and earn the associate's eternal gratitude, but his peers will never forget it.

However, the situation is completely different when it comes to *criticizing* an associate in public. There will be times when you genuinely believe that one of your subordinates needs to be knocked down a peg or two, and that hammering him in a staff meeting is the most dramatic way of making your point.

Think again.

Years ago I happened to be present when a powerful sports official chewed out one of his lieutenants in a meeting that involved only the three of us. Standing his ground, the lieutenant told his boss, "Look, you can criticize me to a third person. You can criticize me to my face. But you can't do it to my face in front of a third person."

The big risk you take in criticizing people in a public forum is that you can't predict their reaction. And the more people present, the more complicated the reaction.

Unless you are absolutely certain that lashing into an employee in front of his peers will achieve the desired effect, save your comments for a one-on-one session. If nothing else, you can then be sure that he will be hearing what's really bothering you rather than worrying about what other people think.

THE OTHER SIDE OF CRITICISM, OR WHAT'S WRONG WITH TOO MUCH PRAISE?

I recently caught up with the son of an old friend over dinner. The young man is in his late twenties and had landed a great job at a major consulting group in New York. His only problem, strangely enough, was dealing with his boss's favorable comments about his performance. It wasn't that his boss was stingy with praise. On the contrary, unlike a lot of bosses, he was more than generous. He said nice things about the young man's work all the time. Yet his praise struck the man as insincere, as if the boss had read some manual about how praise motivates employees.

"I know it sounds strange to knock my boss for praising me," the young man told me, "but I can't help the way I feel. Is it me, or could it be something my boss is doing wrong?"

It's an interesting problem, and it's not necessarily the employee's fault.

I've always thought that praise can be a dangerous motivational tool. A lot of people are clumsy at handing it out.

But even more people are remarkably inept at accepting it. Some people are simply threatened by praise. Perhaps they feel that they don't deserve it, or that they haven't earned it. Perhaps they think it's insincere. Or they don't like the judgment dynamic that comes with praise, a dynamic in which they are forced into a position of being evaluated by someone else, someone who now has power to make them feel good or bad about themselves. It can be perplexing to some people. It's why so many of us deflect the praise that comes our way. We don't think it's addressed to us; we feel it's *aimed* at us. And nobody likes being someone else's target.

People are also uncomfortable with the status implications of praise. A person in a position to say, "You're doing a great job!" (or conversely, "You messed up!") is a person who has, rightfully or not, assumed a position of power over you.

It would be totally inappropriate for you to offer unsolicited commentary on, say, your boss's performance in a sales presentation. You certainly could never critique your boss; that is, you could not say, "You misread the customer in that meeting" or "You forgot to mention our overseas capabilities." Likewise, it would be awkward for you to praise your boss—e.g., "You were terrific in there!" That would be presuming that you had the authority to pass judgment, positive or otherwise.

You have to be invited to offer such commentary. And very few bosses would make the invitation, precisely because of the status instability it creates. The right to praise enrobes them with status and power. And they like to keep that power to themselves. People also sense that they're being "sold" when you praise them (although few of us are acutely aware of it when it is actually happening to us).

40

One of the easiest ways to "seduce" people—whether it's a client, customer, colleague, or future spouse—is to gently but steadily shower them with praise. Compliment them about how they look one day, how they handled a crisis the next day, their taste in music the next, and so on, and pretty soon they will get "addicted" to your compliments. They'll expect them, and they'll miss them when they're withheld. Admiring someone is a strange but surefire technique to win someone's admiration. People will be in your thrall because they think you are enthralled by them.

Inevitably, of course, this seduction begins to pale. No one is perfect. Therefore, no one remains the permanent object of praise. Chinks in the armor always reveal themselves. And the praise is suddenly laced with occasional criticism. If the criticism stings, that's when you know you've been seduced by praise.

I remember a favorite schoolteacher did this to me in my early teens. She was always complimenting me, to the point where, over time, I unconsciously began to regard her adulation as a constant in my scholastic life.

It was great for my youthful self-esteem—until the day I messed up an assignment and she let me know of her displeasure. The criticism stunned me, but more important, it made me realize how dependent I had become on her praise. It didn't change my life, but it taught me a lesson about praise: it is a double-edged sword, and one edge can cut deep. Perhaps the worst feature of praise is that it is usually linked with criticism. You hear this when bosses preface any criticism by telling you, "Everyone is impressed with the job you're doing, *but* your people skills could use a little work." (These bosses' people skills could use a little work, too!) They assume that

41

sprinkling some sugary praise on their critical comments will somehow sweeten the sound of an essentially negative evaluation.

Unfortunately, few people are fooled. They've heard this praise-followed-by-reproof sequence since childhood—from their parents, teachers, and coaches. They know they're being buttered up for the kill. Is it any wonder that people in this situation only hear the bad comments and none of the good? Worse yet, is it any wonder that people doubt the sincerity of the good?

With all these traps built into the concept of praise, I'm not surprised that this particular boss's praise has backfired as a motivational tool. If the young man felt that he was being manipulated, he probably was.

Having said that, however, here's a simple test the young man could have used to make sure that he was not misjudging his boss.

Praise exists largely to express appreciation. But appreciation isn't only expressed to the person being appreciated. It's also shared with others. If you want to gauge your boss's sincerity and feel better about your relationship, find out what he's saying about you to third parties.

The most sincere words are the ones expressed when you're not in the room.

TAPPING THE POWER BURIED IN YOUR FILES

It doesn't take long for people who work with me to realize that I have a great faith in documents and files. In a word, I hoard. I save everything. I have letters, contracts, memos, minutes of meetings, and thank-you notes going back to my first day in business.

None of this makes me unique. I'm sure there are lots of people who are equally incapable of throwing any paper out. But I'm always amazed at how often these same people, who go to such great lengths to maintain complete files, never do anything with their treasure trove of documents. They don't review the documents or refer to them or even let other people know they exist.

(Most puzzling of all, of course, are the people who clean out their files every three or four years when "they take up too much space." Why do they bother saving the files at all if they're only going to junk them when they become a nuisance? How do they know they're unimportant if they never look at them?)

In my opinion, these people are missing out on one of the great tools in a manager's arsenal. There is a tremendous amount of power buried in each executive's files if only more people were willing to tap into it.

The most obvious value of files is the protection they offer you. This is particularly true in a personal services business such as ours where clients have a maddening habit of forgetting all our work on their behalf.

That's one reason I urge all our client managers to maintain what I call "accomplishment files." I ask them to save every document of every good thing they've done for the client, not just the profitable deals they arranged but the marginal or optional services as well (the Barbra Streisand concert tickets for their parents, the free condo for their Mediterranean holiday, etc.). It's good to have such a file when we go to renew our representation agreement with the client. If he gripes that we didn't generate enough money for him, we can show him the eleven lucrative offers that we secured but which he turned down. We can also hand him a paper trail of all the nice-to-have services we provided during the year—as a reminder of how much easier his life has been because of our involvement.

As I say, clients have highly selective memories. An accomplishment file is a great way to correct that flaw and build a stronger relationship.

There's also an "I told you so" element in many files that managers should not be shy about exploiting.

One of my core management devices is my collection of "talk to" files. I maintain a file for each of the seventy or so company executives I talk to on a regular basis. Into these "talk to" files go all the documents—letters to or from the executive, memos to me promising to do something, newspaper clippings, whatever—that I may want to refer to the next time I talk to that executive. I don't remove documents from these files until I'm sure the situation is resolved. It's not unusual for me to go through a "talk to" file and find letters that go back two decades but are still potential opportunities in my mind.

For example, one of our executives has been strenuously arguing that we should be developing a relationship with a major media company. In going through this executive's "talk to" file, I was amused to find three memos from me to him about this company, dating back to 1982. The 1982 memo was a one-liner attached to a *Forbes* magazine profile of this up-and-coming company, which asked, "Are we talking to these people?" A 1986 memo was attached to another magazine profile of the company's CEO and inquired what we should be doing with him. The third memo from 1987, attached to yet another major profile, asked more strenuously, "Are we going to be there when this group starts buying sports programming?"

At the appropriate moment (probably the next time this executive urges me to meet with this CEO), I intend to haul out these memos. Yes, there's a little bit of "I told you so" in this gesture, but I'm not trying to rub it in this man's face. My real goal is common-sense management. I want to put an exclamation point on my view of our business and the direction we should be taking. The next time I ask something, I don't want to wait twelve years before something happens. I want him to trust my instincts and act on my suggestion right away. I suspect these three "forgotten" memos will make that point (and make it quickly, painlessly, and amicably) in a way that few other management techniques can.

I couldn't do that if I didn't save the documents and refer back to them once in a while.

There are some other very positive benefits when a manager retrieves an ancient memo that still has some relevance to the company. Passing around a twelve-year-old document demonstrates your meticulousness. It's concrete proof of your memory, your thoughtfulness, or the fact that you let very few things fall through the cracks. People may react in different ways to this maneuver—some will be awestruck, some irritated, some embarrassed that they forgot it—but I have to believe that it's good for employees to hear their boss's footsteps once in a while.

I've yet to discover an easier way of achieving these ends than tapping the power buried in your files.

ARE YOU RUBBING PEOPLE THE WRONG WAY?

One of our executives was briefing me about a decisionmaker I was about to call on. He described the decisionmaker as a "scratchy personality."

"I don't know what it is about him," said our executive, "but he rubs everyone the wrong way."

Before I left my initial meeting with the man, I could see what our executive meant. He had all the attributes of someone who would go far. He was smart and articulate. He dressed well. He had attended prestigious schools, lived on the best street in the most exclusive suburb, belonged to the "right" clubs, and wasn't shy about letting you know who his influential friends were. I suppose that was the rub—within thirty minutes of meeting me, he had made sure I knew all the wonderful things he had going for him.

This fellow was way too pleased with himself. Unless he learns to tone down his incessant self promotion, he might not go as far in life as he expects.

I think each one of us has at least a few personality defects that rub people the wrong way, and in turn diminish us in others' eyes and perhaps hold back our careers.

For example, I am ruthless about separating my personal life from my business life. (See "When It's Nobody's Business But Your Own" on page 120.) I don't hobnob with company employees after hours, largely because you can't go out on the town with someone and then turn him down for a raise the next morning. I'm sure this has made me appear more distant, more uninterested in people than I probably deserve. Perhaps it has even cost me the loyalty of some employees over the years.

The good news is that I know this about myself. Keeping the two areas separate is a conscious decision I made long ago, with rewards that I believe outweigh the consequences.

The bad news for many people is that they have no idea how they are coming across to others. Even worse, they're oblivious to the consequences of their shortcomings.

Consider the following quirks which may be costing you more than you realize.

1. ARE YOU ALWAYS "FAR TOO BUSY"?

Some people can't help letting you know how busy they are. They always have a pile of phone messages on their desk and a stack of documents that need reading. They are always whizzing past you, late for a meeting or running to catch a plane. If you need a moment of their time, they promise to fit you in real soon—and then, often, they never do.

I don't care how busy you are, if you *can't* make time for the people who need you, then you're not really busy, you're just disorganized. If you *don't* make time for these same people, eventually they will stop coming to you and you will have lost some valuable allies. For what? To make another meeting, catch another plane, answer another call, dash off another memo?

2. DO YOU SEEK ADVICE AND IGNORE IT?

This is the flip side of being far too busy or not having enough time. If you ask someone for advice and then, without explanation, ignore it, you have wasted their time. Do this on a regular basis and you will have needlessly lost a friend.

3. ARE YOU JEKYLL OR HYDE?

Some people pride themselves on being able to work in furious spurts. These are the Jekyll and Hyde types, who are emotionally up one day and down the next. The problem, of course, is that colleagues find this disorienting. They never know which way the Jekyll and Hyde persona's emotional arrow is pointing. And the effort to find out is usually not worth it. Nobody likes to be completely predictable, but there is something to be said for consistency— for being able to react with solid judgment to the day-to-day crises that crop up in every business. It brands you as reliable. There's no such thing as being reliable only some of the time.

4. Do you argue too much?

An adversarial streak is valuable in a lawyer or negotiator. Employers and clients will pay you handsomely to do their arguing for them. But nobody likes an argumentative person out of context. If you find yourself arguing with everyone who walks through your door, you might be better off closing the door until you change your ways.

5. Are you nervous, energetic, or both?

Some people have a lot of nervous energy. They can't sit still. They flit around the office and make a general nuisance of themselves, always bothering people at the wrong moment. People with too much nervous energy don't energize their colleagues; they just get on their nerves.

6. Do you tread with a big foot?

I read a quote once by a major TV personality claiming that she doesn't like to "big foot" a program she is working on. That is, she doesn't need to leave her superstar footprints on every aspect of the show. She doesn't use her power to dominate the producers, writers, and directors. That sort of restraint is rare and admirable.

Too many people think that because they have power in an organization, they are obliged to exercise it—in every situation.

A few years back I asked one of our senior executives to help out on a project. Because of his rank or his forceful personality, he proceeded to take over the project. Unfortunately, he dominated the project into the ground. All the other people lost their enthusiasm when they started feeling his big footprints on their back. They abandoned him and, in turn, the project. In the long run he came out the loser. People would have respected him more if he had played his supporting role rather than exercised his star privileges.

THE PROPER WAY TO PLAY YOUR SUPPORTING ROLE

One of the strengths of our company, I believe, is that our people rarely confuse themselves with our athlete clients. We know our role is important, but still it is a supporting role. The clients are the ones who are out there on the playing field creating success; it's our job to manage the fruits of that success.

I recall a chilling occasion when two of the more experienced executives in our company forgot to play their supporting role.

The incident involved a female executive at a major advertising agency who had invited us to explain the benefits of sports marketing to her biggest account, a Boston-based computer maker.

The meeting got off to a rocky start the moment our executives pulled up in a stretch limousine. I don't personally object to limousines; when you're on a tight schedule they're often the most cost-efficient and practical method of transportation. But apparently the ad executive and her client did. They thought the limo was ostentatious and not a good sign about how we allocate our resources.

As a piece of communication—that is, as a gesture that sent out a message—it made a bad first impression. Our executives should have known better.

Things went downhill from there. As soon as everyone settled in their seats, our executives took over. They were very intent on impressing the computer manufacturer that we were *the* pros in sports marketing. Their presentation was dazzling and the computer maker was impressed.

Unfortunately, none of this mattered in the long run— because the ad executive who had arranged the meeting felt shut out. Our executives had so thoroughly dominated the meeting that they alienated her. We had forgotten to play our supporting role and, consequently, had made an adversary for life. Our company has yet to do any business with either the computer maker or the ad agency—and I now have a good idea why.

I recall a situation several years ago that had a more happy ending for us. We were approached by representatives of a popular athlete about handling his commercial endorsements. This athlete had a team of advisers—one to handle his legal work, another to oversee his day-to-day affairs, still another to manage his finances and investments. It seemed needlessly complicated to us, but who were we to argue? After all, it was this trio of advisers who had brought the athlete to our door. So we began working for him.

However, as we delved into the athlete's affairs we sensed that his financial adviser was not doing a good job.

Now, our normal impulse in this situation would be to alert the client. That's the right thing to do. But in this case, that would have been counterproductive. For one thing, it wasn't any of our business. Furthermore, it was no way to treat a friend who brought us into the relationship, even someone who was out of his league. And chances are, if we had taken swipes at the adviser, the athlete would have backed him rather than us.

Instead, we bided our time and kept silent. Whenever the athlete expressed dissatisfaction with his financial management, we would sort of agree with him, yet never actually say anything disparaging. Within a year, the athlete came to the desired conclusion. The adviser was gone and we were managing his finances.

If someone is shepherding you into a client relationship or helping you capitalize on their contacts, you must be very sensitive to that relationship. No matter how skilled you are at communicating your abilities and achievements, you sometimes have to bite your tongue and hold back. You can never put the people who are helping you in a bad light. That's the proper way to play a supporting role.

CHAPTER 3

It All Begins with the Words You Choose

My Favorite Words

I once heard a psychologist who is an expert on relationships
offer a theory that a woman can learn everything she needs to
know about her future husband by taking the man to a restaurant.

"How he treats a waitress," said this psychologist, "is how
he'll treat you."

You can extend this point about insight in unexpected
places to almost any situation in or out of business. I've gained
insights into people's personalities on the tennis court (if they
always give the close line calls to themselves, they'll probably
give themselves the benefit of the doubt on a deal point, too)
and on the golf course (if they stretch the truth about their

53

score they're probably just as creative with the facts of a transaction).

I've also formed lasting impressions about people at work—by observing how they deal with my secretaries, by noting the kind of people they claim as "friends" in business, by monitoring how well they can keep a secret, or by clocking their response time to a request from their *least-important* client.

As a manager, I've spent years watching people, testing them, assessing their behavior in stressful situations, and looking for tendencies and patterns, all in an effort to form and reform my opinions. I have to do this. It's an essential survival mechanism in a world that changes rapidly.

But in all my years of looking for insight in odd places, there's one area that I've virtually ignored: how people communicate in writing. And yet people's written communication is probably more revealing than any other single item in the workplace.

This struck me as such an obvious oversight that I decided to test it out on myself. I analyzed several years of my memos and letters, looking for recurring subjects and words.

I confirmed a couple of things about myself that I probably already knew. For example, I learned that the people I regarded as most important in my personal life and in my business were the people I most frequently communicated with in writing. There was virtually a direct correlation between an individual's importance to me and how often I wrote to that person. (This shouldn't be remarkable. It should be true of everyone in business. Yet I wonder how many people neglect to communicate as frequently as they should with the people whom they regard as most important.)

I also learned that I rely heavily on memos and letters during crises. There were periods when my writing activity increased dramatically, and those writing periods corresponded directly with times of the year when we were facing stiff challenges in some parts of our company. (This, too, makes sense. When you're in a tough situation, you want to communicate as broadly as possible to marshal maximum support and to make sure everyone is on the same page.)

By far the most revealing lesson was the list of my favorite words. The following words pop up repeatedly in my memos and letters:

- Credibility

- Responsive

- Follow-up

- Timely

- Proactive

- Expenses

- Profit

- Fair

- Aggressive

- Extraordinary

- Opportunity

In my mind, it's a flattering list—although I'm not sure everyone would agree. Each word reveals a part of me and provides an accurate glimpse of how I see myself as a businessman. For example:

- *Credibility*: This is the "sports agent" part of me. I've always fought against the image of an agent as some finger-snapping, fast-talking fly-by-night wearing an open shirt with gold chains who's here today and gone tomorrow. I wanted to project an image of stability and credibility—someone who's in it for the long term.

- *Responsive*: This is the lawyer in me, dotting every *i* and crossing every *t*, addressing each issue immediately because I know that if I let anything slide by, it will ultimately blow up in my face.

- *Follow-up*: This is the salesman in me, the part that knows you never close a deal on the first or second try, but you do if you follow up persistently and habitually.

- *Timely*: This is the efficiency expert in me, which knows that effective follow-up and responsiveness are meaningless if they're not done on time as promised.

- *Proactive*: This is the sales manager in me, which understands that some salespeople are simply order takers. But if you want your business to grow, you need people who know how to make things happen and you need to reward their initiative and ingenuity.

- *Expenses*: This is the manager in me, the one who realizes how costs can spiral out of control in a dynamic business and who always wants our income to exceed (if only slightly) our expenses.

- *Profit*: This is the entrepreneur in me who's neither ashamed to

make a profit nor afraid to quote a big number to ensure that
profit on every project.

- *Fair:* This is another of my entrepreneurial sides, which recognizes that if I deserve a decent profit in a transaction, the other
  party does too.

- *Aggressive:* This is the competitor in me, which plays hard and
  to win.

- *Extraordinary:* This is the salesman in me, which occasionally
  overpraises the product or service I'm selling. In my experience, it's not enough to believe in the product or service, you
  have to believe it's the best.

- *Opportunity:* This is the risk taker in me, the one who's eternally
  optimistic, and sees a chance to succeed where others see a
  chance to fail, and is constantly encouraging people to see it my
  way.

If I had the time and energy, I suppose I could apply the same
analysis to the memos and letters business associates send me.
If nothing else, the words they use repeatedly would give me
a clue about how they see themselves and what they think of
doing business with me.

But the more important lesson here is one of self examination. All of us could learn something by studying our writing habits. We'd not only learn if we are communicating as
often as we should with the people who really matter, but
whether our various writings give an accurate picture of what
we think of others and, most important, what we think of
ourselves.

Words don't lie. If you haven't stepped back to examine the words you use day in and day out, isn't it time you did?

FOUR PHRASES I CAN LIVE WITHOUT

All of us have verbal tics, little phrases that populate our everyday conversation. Most are harmless if not meaningless. For example, when people say "Wow" upon hearing a mundane news bulletin, they are uttering an automatic response that, after numbing repetition, becomes trite. "Wow" no longer connotes enthusiasm and wide-eyed astonishment. It's no better than nodding your head or muttering, "Uh huh."

Some tics are merely irritating. For example, it seems that half the people under the age of thirty that I meet today cannot answer a question without repeating it. It's a tic that buys them time to formulate an answer, although I doubt its young practitioners are aware that they're even doing it. If they were, they'd stop this annoyance that adds a needless echo to a simple dialogue.

Some tics are very revealing. I know one executive who is fond of ending his more halfhearted suggestions with the phrase, "It's a beautiful thing." It's as if he expects this upbeat flourish will convince me or his other colleagues that he knows what he's talking about. I've learned over time that it means the opposite, that it's a signal to probe deeper. If he doesn't believe in the idea, why should I?

Some verbal tics, however, are more pernicious, especially when they are spoken by people who are aware of what they're doing. That's when a harmless or annoying tic graduates into a phrase I can live without. Here are a handful to beware:

1. "To be perfectly honest with you . . ."

This may be the most abused phrase in the workplace. It doesn't bother me for the obvious reason, namely, the implication that all preceding remarks were less than honest. I don't think that's true. The people who use this phrase are not liars. But their statements might be sloppy and inaccurate.

Whenever I hear this phrase, I can't help thinking that this is the first time in our conversation that the other person is being serious, alert, and precise with me—and that everything else he or she said might be suspect.

I realize people say "To be perfectly honest with you . . ." without thinking. But doesn't it suggest the possibility that they aren't thinking much about anything else they say either?

2. "I shouldn't be telling you this."

That's right, you shouldn't.

What worries me here is not so much that a person is breaking a confidence (there are often legitimate reasons to do so), but rather that he or she is announcing the fact fully aware that it's better not to do so. It's like knowing that robbing a bank is against the law—but robbing the bank anyway. Acknowledging that you're committing a crime doesn't mean you can go ahead and do it.

Wouldn't it be better simply to announce that the shared secret is "just between the two of us" and leave it at that?

You've made the point that you're sharing a confidence, without suggesting that you're breaking someone else's.

3. "THE FACT OF THE MATTER IS . . ."

People who abuse this phrase may as well hold up a sign saying, "Beware! Lecture Approaching." They're clearing their throat, sweeping aside everything you've said because it's wrong or misinformed, and preparing to instruct you on the real truth (as they perceive it).

Sometimes they're right. Sometimes they're clueless. But I don't know anyone who likes hearing it.

In the hands of a skilled debater and used no more than once in any meeting, this phrase can be a terrific rhetorical device. It can totally wipe out the other side's position, especially if you have marshaled a brilliant set of facts immediately after saying, "The fact of the matter is . . . "

But too often people say it without any supporting facts. At those moments, it can backfire. A phrase designed to make the other side feel less smart can end up making the speaker look stupid.

4. "WE TRIED THAT ONCE BEFORE AND . . ."

Some people instinctively respond to any new idea by comparing it to something in the past and finding it lacking by comparison. "We tried that once before . . ." is a phrase that identifies colleagues who think this way.

That's good and bad.

It's good to have people inside a company who function as your "institutional memory." When everyone in the room is excited by a seemingly new idea, it's valuable to have an iconoclast there who can remind everyone that (a) the idea is not new, (b) the company tried it eight years earlier, and (c) these are the reasons it failed. If that is the start of an intense discussion about why the idea could succeed today, then "We tried that once before . . ." is the start of something good.

But it's bad when "We tried that once before . . ." is the automatic and first response to any suggestion, with no institutional memory to support it. In those cases, the phrase indicates a "been there, done that" attitude that can kill any semblance of entrepreneurial vigor in an organization.

I can't count the number of times I hear familiar ideas being touted as fresh and new in the course of a normal business week. It's an occupational hazard of being in business for thirty-five years. Eventually, every concept begins to seem like *déjà vu* all over again. But I don't automatically express my feelings. I bite my tongue and let the sponsors of an idea present their case. If I'm going to say, "We've tried that once before . . ." I'd rather it came at the end of a meeting (after I've heard all the facts) rather than at the start (when I haven't heard any).

LOOKING OUT FOR NUMBER ONE WITHOUT OVERLOOKING EVERYONE ELSE

The ability to assert yourself is surely one of the more valuable assets in business when you consider how often assertiveness is required during the course of a business day. These moments happen everywhere—in an airport, a ticket line, at home, and in the office.

Let's say a colleague vigorously opposes you in a staff meeting (a common occurrence). Do you let it slide, telling yourself that everyone in the room knows your position, that this colleague is out of line, and that you won't dignify his comments with a response?

Do you forcefully defend yourself on the spot, not wishing to appear weak in front of your coworkers?

Or do you bide your time, cornering the attacker later on in private and setting him straight?

Depending on the circumstances, any one of these responses is appropriate. There are times when silly people do make inane arguments, and responding to them will only make you look silly. You're better off biting your tongue and letting their shots glance off you. Likewise, there are times when someone has scored a knockdown and you have to come up swinging.

Most often, though, you should wait. Pick your battle. Assert yourself when the timing is best for you, not the other guy.

Unfortunately, many people get this sort of assertiveness wrong. They think that any opposition from subordinates or peers is a challenge to their authority or judgment and must be counteracted immediately. This can be dangerous, especially in a workplace where others are also assertive.

Actually, in many circumstances, the unconventional and less assertive approach may be far more effective. Constantly standing your ground and waging war with real or imagined adversaries is exhausting. It's also not a good way to deal with people. As the saying goes, "When your only tool is a hammer, everyone looks like a nail."

The most successful people know that it's far less costly to disarm your opposition than to engage them in battle. It's also very easy. In a crisis or confrontational situation, often an apt phrase or elegant sentence is all you need to win the day. Here are four ways to communicate your position without bullying or offending people:

1. "I UNDERSTAND YOUR PROBLEM."

This is the sweetest sounding sentence you can introduce into a potentially tense situation. It not only makes you appear sympathetic, but it disarms the other side. In one fell swoop, you have positioned yourself as an ally rather than an adversary. Use these four words the next time you're facing a disappointed customer who wants his money back or an airline ticket clerk who has the power to determine whether you make or miss an overbooked flight.

2. "I AGREE, BUT . . ."

The gentlest way to defuse your opposition in a tense negotiation or an in-house test of wills is to agree with their position and then cancel it out. The use of the conjunction "but" is invaluable here: "I know exactly what you mean, but . . ." This conveys the impression that you have accepted the other side's position, when in fact you have done nothing more than acknowledge it.

Most people use this technique every day without realizing it. The really successful people know precisely when they are using it, and why.

3. POKE FUN AT YOURSELF BEFORE THEY DO.

Self-deprecation is the least offensive and least obvious way of asserting yourself. After all, once you have poked fun at yourself there is no need for the other side to do so.

For example, in a restaurant, if I want a particular table or extra ice in my glass, I will say, "I know you think I'm crazy, but I really like sitting on the left side of the room," or "This may seem absurd to you, but can I have three glasses of ice cubes." This is far better than dictating, "I must have the left corner table!" or "Give me three glasses of ice!" which only incites other people to think "What a jerk!" or "Who do you think you are?" The self-deprecatory approach eliminates that because you have already admitted that it is a dumb or unusual request. You have literally taken the words out of their mouth.

4. BLAME THE CHAIR.

Since ego is at the root of nearly all tense situations, whenever possible do or say something to defuse your ego or theirs before addressing the more substantive issues. One of the best techniques is to depersonalize the situation, i.e., blame it on *something* rather than *someone*.

Peter Jennings, the on-camera star of ABC News and the anchor of the network's daily evening news broadcast, was preparing to broadcast a studio discussion with three ABC correspondents. Jennings, who is nearly 6' 2", was seated next to his colleague and long-time White House correspondent Brit Hume, who is an inch taller. Keenly aware of his on-camera "stature" as anchorman, Jennings turned to an assistant and said, "I think this chair probably wants to come up a bit." A small thing, perhaps, but delicately effective. In one sentence, Jennings depersonalized a display of ego. Instead of exercising his prerogative as the star, he made the chair the culprit.

CHAPTER 4

The Games People Play
With the Truth

I was once invited to dine at the offices of an executive I had known off and on for many years. The luncheon was served in an elegant room next to the executive's office. It was an inordinately formal four-course affair, served by a chef attired in a white jacket who would enter with each new course from a hidden door. The conversation was intriguing. The meal was splendid. The whole experience seemed choreographed to soothe guests and impress them.

I know that I was impressed—not only by the executive's hospitality but by the fact that he seemed to have a full-time kitchen at his disposal. He had come a long way since I first knew him.

At the end of the meal, as the chef refilled our cups of coffee, the host reinforced the impression. He praised the chef on the richness of the meal, patted his stomach, and jovially added, "I'm glad I'm not eating here this evening."

A nice touch, I thought. He had made sure I knew he had a chef on staff day and night.

I later learned that the meal was, in fact, brought in by a catering service and that the chef worked for the caterer.

But that didn't diminish my appreciation of his effort. I was particularly impressed by how artfully he had played with the truth to suggest the chef was on staff. He hadn't said anything that was an outright lie. He didn't have to. He had simply timed his remarks and omitted certain facts to achieve the desired effect. It was more a sin of omission than commission.

This little episode is just one of the many games people play with the truth each day. I don't necessarily endorse this man's verbal sleight of hand, but it's hard to condemn it, because all of us play games with the truth dozens of times each day. We usually don't have any other choice. Consider these five scenarios that may be familiar to you.

1. WHEN THE TRUTH HURTS

Let's say a friend has just received a bad haircut and asks you, "How do I look?"

How would you respond?

Most people would fib or use a euphemism that gets them off the hook. Instinct tells them there's no reward for telling the truth. All you've done is hurt a friend.

The fact is, complete honesty is a perpetual risk/reward decision. What do you gain by telling the truth and what do you stand to lose if you shade it a little bit in your favor? Even the most saintly and scrupulous among us play this game.

For example, most people who find twenty-five cents on the floor of a movie theater would put it in their pocket—because the effort of returning it is not worth twenty-five cents, nor is there any risk or reward in doing so. No one will be grateful for the rescue of a quarter and no one will think ill of you for keeping it.

However, if you found $25,000 on the floor, you still might pocket it but you'd think about returning it or locating the rightful owner. The rewards and risks are much greater. Someone will be grateful if you do the right thing. And a lot of people might regard it as inexcusable if it turns out that you didn't.

2. WHEN AN ERROR NEEDS CONCEALING

Most people play games with the truth in order to conceal an error or failure to do something. If they're late for a meeting, miss a deadline, or need to cancel lunch with a friend, they'll make up an excuse that isn't likely to be challenged.

People also tend to fiddle with the truth when they are dealing with a computer. I see this all the time on business travel. A harried executive needs to make a particular flight but forgot to make a reservation. He has two options: He can rush up to the ticket counter, admit that he doesn't have a reservation, and place himself at the ticket agent's mercy. Or he can blame the computer: "I made a reservation," he says. "It was confirmed." The risk is minimal. The reward is tangible: Blaming the computer makes the agent try a little harder to get him on that flight. If the flight is really important, a lot of people might stretch the truth to make it.

3. When it's the most convenient excuse

People also use phony pretexts to avoid work. I do that with people who send me their book manuscripts so I can provide a jacket quote. Unless they are a friend, I always say, "My publisher won't let me do that because it conflicts with sales of my book." The truth is I'd rather not go to the trouble of coming up with a quote, nor do I have the time or inclination to read their book. But saying that to someone, even a stranger, is socially graceless. It's more candor than most people can handle.

4. When there's no visual evidence

The telephone probably generates the most white lies in business—because you can say virtually anything and the person on the other end of the line has no visual evidence to disprove you. If I think the timing is not to my advantage to take someone's call, I will instruct my secretary, "Tell them I'm on an overseas call. I'll get back to them." (I do call back when the time is right for me.) That excuse sounds better than telling them I haven't got the time or that I'm doing something more important than their call.

5. When no one can dispute you

Sometimes playing with the truth can make you look good. For example, recreational tennis is a sport where, if you let it, every line call can become a struggle with the truth. The obvious solution is to call the lines exactly as you see them.

But it's tricky. Which way do you go when you think the ball might be out but you didn't see it clearly? It depends on what's at stake. If winning at all costs is crucial to you, you might call it in your favor—damn the impression it makes.

On the other hand, if your opponent is a potential customer and you are trying to impress him with your fairness, you might give him the benefit of the doubt. You might legitimately say, "I didn't see it but it was probably in." Do this consistently on the close calls and you can soar in your opponent's estimation. He'll not only like you, he'll want to do business with you because he can rely on you to give the close calls in business to him.

Candor Comes in Many Forms

I think a lot of business people have a problem with candor. Perhaps that's because so many of us put a premium on secrecy and finesse in business.

In a sales situation, we tend to highlight our product or service's virtues rather than its liabilities.

In a negotiation, we take pride in being able to disclose information when it's to our advantage rather than the other side's.

In managing people, we prefer to give them only as much information as we feel they need. In other words, we make a virtue of our ability to obscure a situation.

Of course, that's not all bad. We all face situations when being less than candid is the most prudent course of action (and inflicts no damage to our conscience and ethical well-being). A car salesman, for example, is not necessarily obliged

71

to tell a customer that the model he is admiring in the show-room is rated fourth in its class in gas mileage. That's not candor; it's bad salesmanship. Why steer customers to the competition?

But all this emphasis on being less than candid perhaps blinds us to the considerable virtues of candor itself.

Candor comes in many guises.

The most common, of course, is the crude, blunt variety. You tell people exactly what you're thinking, and hope they appreciate your honesty.

When in doubt, I am a very frank person. If I have done something wrong, I admit it. If I am mad, I say so. If I am disappointed, I let people know it. This sort of candor is not only good therapy for my conscience and spirit, but I've noticed that it has a cleansing effect on some of the messiest situations. Sunshine, as they say, is the best disinfectant.

The best time to employ this sort of candor is when you have made a mistake.

People generally have two options when they are in a jam: They can try to obscure the situation, or they can open their soul and tell the truth. Candor is the better option.

If you can be candid with people in the moments when you have achieved far less than your best, you'll find that they are more likely (a) to remember your candor instead of your trespasses, (b) to forgive you, and (c) to be equally candid with you.

Candor is particularly valuable when you are competing for new business against other people. It sets you apart from the crowd, because most people are not as candid as they should be about what they have done or can do. Jean-Claude Killy once told me that a big reason he agreed to become our client back in 1967 (when I was still in my thirties and had virtually no presence in skiing or in Europe) was that I never promised him anything, whereas everyone else who was pursuing him was promising him the world.

Then there are the more subtle forms of candor—where the situation requires that you charm rather than bludgeon people with your honesty.

I owe this piece of advice to my good friend, Gordon Forbes, who played Davis Cup tennis for South Africa in the 1950s and 1960s just before the professional era began. At the end of his amateur career, out of necessity, Forbes found a "real" job selling industrial lighting fixtures in Johannesburg.

Forbes started out with very small orders, but one day he was asked to bid on a huge contract to supply all the interior lighting for a mining project. He spent days writing the proposal, right up to the deadline, and submitted it with great apprehension.

The next day, the mining company summoned him to a meeting to discuss it. Forbes took this as a positive sign, but the company assured him that all bidders were being consulted.

In a conference room filled with mining engineers, Forbes listened as they explained that, in price and quality, his bid was identical to all the others. One engineer even suggested that the price had been fixed among the bidders, which Forbes firmly denied.

The engineer then lowered the boom. "Can you give us any reasons at all why this corporation should favor your fittings ahead of those offered by your competitors?" he asked.

Forbes was dumbfounded. His mind raced for an answer, but none was forthcoming.

Then he remembered the great Australian player, Roy Emerson, who for a time on the tour had adopted the endearing affectation of doing everything "with feeling." If Emerson hit a great passing shot, it was hit "with feeling." If a steak was particularly tasty, it was served "with feeling."

With this in mind, Forbes stared down the engineers and said, "Gentlemen, have you taken into account the fact that each one of our light fittings will be delivered to you with feeling?"

The room broke up with laughter. Even Forbes's harshest interrogator allowed that his reason had some validity though "of a nontechnical nature." He won the contract.

Forbes eventually parlayed this first big sale into the largest lighting company in the southern hemisphere.

But I think his response was the most subtle form of candor, so subtle, in fact, that the other side perhaps didn't realize it. The engineer had asked him a trick question—no different than the "Why should I hire you?" question that interviewers always pose to nervous job applicants—and Forbes had responded in kind, with a clever trick answer.

Humor is perhaps the best form of candor, because it not only delivers a message but makes everyone feel good about hearing it. As such, it can unstick a lot of sticky situations.

I recall a few months back, the chairman of a leading British shipping company was talking to his long-time bank about financing a major acquisition. Minutes into the meeting it was apparent to the chairman and the half-dozen bankers who had gathered there that the bank did not have the resources or expertise to handle the acquisition.

It was an awkward moment for the chairman. Not only did he feel a sense of loyalty to the bankers, but he didn't enjoy the prospect of having to cut off the meeting abruptly and inform them that they were in over their head.

Instead, the chairman launched into a joke about a young man walking down a London street who is confronted by a lady of the night.

"Hello sweetie," said the lady. "How would you like to spend some time with me?"

"Well, there are three reasons I can't do that," the young man explained. "First, I don't have any money."

"I don't need to hear the other two reasons," said the lady and walked away.

The bankers laughed, the message sunk in, and the meeting ended a few minutes thereafter.

THE TERRIBLE TRUTH ABOUT SECRETS

A Swiss executive once told me that he judged people almost exclusively by how well they could keep a secret.

"If they can keep a secret," he said, "they are my friends for life. If they can't, I don't regard them as human beings. They are merely tools to be used for my own purposes, but I will never trust them."

I thought this gentleman's attitude was exceedingly severe and simplistic. The ability to keep a secret may be a highly prized character trait, but you can't divide the world into people who can keep a secret and people who can't. Life is more complicated than that.

If on a scale of 1 to 10, your company's payroll manager (who knows everyone's paycheck but never reveals it) is a 10 at keeping secrets and the indiscriminate gossip down the hall whom no one in their right mind would trust is a 1, then most of us fall into the numbers in between.

Some factors to consider before you rush to judgment.

1. IS IT BROADCAST NEWS?

I'm convinced that the great majority of the secrets that are revealed to us—even those of a delicate personal nature— are not really secrets at all. People have motives for disclosing them to us, usually with the expectation that we will broadcast them.

For example, a colleague at work tells you that he's having trouble at home, that he and his wife are getting divorced. That's delicate information. But is it a secret? Or is it simply a quick, convenient way for your colleague to bring his marital troubles out into the open without having to endure the pain of repeating it to a dozen different people.

If you spread that secret around, who's to say that you can't be trusted? You might actually be doing your colleague a big favor.

2. WHAT'S THE RELATIONSHIP?

The significance of a secret is usually determined by the relationship of the people who share it.

The secrets between husband and wife, for example, are virtually sacred. Betraying such a confidence is often unforgivable.

In the workplace, you will find equally sacrosanct secrets between executives and their secretaries. Bosses expect their secretaries to be paragons of discretion. As in a marriage, disclosing any secret without the boss's permission is tantamount to treason—and cause for dismissal.

Likewise with secrets that arise out of the relationship between buyer and seller. Whether they're buying plumbing fixtures or sponsorship of a sports event, customers expect their suppliers to be totally guarded about the volume, price, and business strategy behind their purchases. That sort of confidentiality is either tacit or written into the sales agreement, but a successful supplier knows not to cross that line. The converse also applies: If I'm selling electrical wiring to my best customer for $2 a foot less than anyone else is getting, that's the sort of trade secret I expect that customer to keep to himself. I certainly don't want him to disclose it to my other customers.

The bonds of trust are looser when it comes to secrets among coworkers. I'm not sure why—perhaps because peer-to-peer or boss-to-subordinate relationships are more vaguely defined or the secrets they traffic in are less sensitive—but I do know that when colleagues share a secret they usually preface it by saying, "This is confidential" or "Don't tell anyone"—whereas in closer relationships that sentiment is understood.

3. WHERE'S THE CRIME?

Sometimes you become privy to secrets that involve such outrageous behavior that betraying the confidence seems like a minor indiscretion.

A few years ago one of our competitors wrote a letter to
a foreign television network packaging the TV rights to several events that we represented. Our competitor had no right
to do that.

I learned about it because a friend at the foreign network, in strictest confidence, showed me the letter. Even
though the letter itself was unethical (and possibly criminal)
and had a direct impact on me, my friend did not want it revealed that he was passing network "secrets" to me.

For months I wavered about what to do with the letter.
Should I show it to people in the business to punish my com-
petitor? Or keep it in my desk to protect my network friend?
Eventually the letter was made public through another source.
But I cannot honestly say that I would have kept that secret
forever.

4. IS THERE A THIRD PARTY?

The hardest secrets to keep tend to involve a third party who
would be better off knowing what you already know.

For example, in high school, your best friend Joe tells
you that he plans to ask Suzy out on an expensive date. But
Suzy has privately told you that she's not romantically interested in Joe.

Do you tell Joe and spare him the embarrassment of being rejected by Suzy? Or do you keep Suzy's confidence and let
your best friend fend for himself?

This may seem like a trivial crisis of adolescence, but
similar scenarios occur all the time in business. An associate
at another company tells you that he plans to sink a large sum
of money into an investment that, through privileged sources,
you know is doomed to fail. Do you share that secret information with him or keep it to yourself and watch him lose
his shirt?

A friendly rival in the sports business once told me that
he was getting on a plane to go to Europe to make a last-ditch
effort to represent a sports event. The trip would cost him
several thousand dollars, which he could barely afford at the
time. I happened to know—again, in confidence and before the
news would be made public—that the event's organizers were
already with someone else, namely us. Would you tell a rival
that he was wasting his money? Or keep the secret to yourself?
In this case, I advised him to stay home. I couldn't see anyone
(other than the airline) benefiting from my ability to keep
that secret. So I let it out.

The terrible truth about secrets is that keeping them is not
always honorable and revealing them is not always ignoble.

ARE YOU GABBING UP OR DOWN?

I once conducted an informal survey of mid-level employees
about what they regarded as the single most critical attribute
of a leader they would be willing to follow. The answers went
all over the place but generally focused on qualities such as

79

brainpower, courage, and fairness. A leader, I was told, had to be a little smarter than the troops, tough but fair in making decisions (rather than biased or overemotional), willing to take risks, and cool in a crisis.

It was hard to argue with those answers, but when I asked several CEOs what they regarded as the most important requirement for someone in their leadership position, they all said the same thing: The ability to maintain a confidence.

It's a fascinating distinction. The troops admire their bosses for the qualities that everyone can see—brains, guts, and grace under pressure. The bosses, on the other hand, believe their authority stems from a quality that very few people, including their own employees, can recognize.

There's a reason for this, of course. The ability to keep a confidence is not obvious. It doesn't call attention to itself. You only notice it when it is absent—that is, when someone has betrayed your trust.

But I'm convinced that, over time, the ability to maintain a confidence provides would-be leaders with more subtle benefits than almost any other attribute. For one thing, it makes you better informed. People are more willing to tell you their "secrets" when they know you won't share them with anyone else. This is true whether the secrets are coming to you from your customers, clients, bosses, or subordinates—that is, from high, low, or to the side. Given the choice, people will always gravitate to a tight-lipped individual than to a gabby one. And with secrets, everyone does have a choice.

If that ability to earn people's trust and confidence isn't the defining mark of a leader, I don't know what is.

Developing this attribute (and the reputation for being trustworthy) shouldn't be tough. In theory, all you have to

do is keep your mouth shut. When you find yourself beginning sentences with "I shouldn't be telling you this . . ." stop
yourself and rethink the consequences. People may appreciate the fact that you are sharing confidential information with
them, but at the same time, they're wondering what secrets
about them you may be sharing with the rest of the world.

Keeping your mouth shut is nice in theory, but the reality is that most people can't do it, even though common sense
tells them they should. In a society where information is power
and the value of a piece of information is in direct propor-
tion to how few people know it, people think they have to
give out information in order to get information. The irony of
this "I'll show you mine if you show me yours" philosophy is
that it's simply not true. In my experience, the less information you give, the more people entrust with you—precisely
because they know it will not go beyond you.

Think about it: Who would you rather turn to with a
confidential problem? Someone who'll keep your secret or
someone who'll spread it around? And what difference does it
make if that person doesn't share a secret of his or her own with
you? There's no *quid pro quo* with secrets.

I realize that not everyone can keep a secret, that not
every secret is meant to be kept (where would political journalists be without leaked information?), and that not everything should remain a secret (particularly when revealing it
helps someone without doing anyone else harm). Somewhere
within this maze of contradictions is a happy medium.

My solution is to be extremely discriminating about the
people with whom I share a confidence or proprietary information and even more discriminating about the people with whom

I share someone else's secrets. The former is a tight circle of friends and confidantes; the latter is an even tighter circle.

In theory, this should be an easy policy to practice, but reality catches up with a lot of people. A friend of mine calls this the difference between "gabbing up and gabbing down." As he sees it, the problem is not so much the betrayal of a confidence, but rather the betrayal is done with the wrong person.

It's one thing to share privileged information with an individual—a friend, customer, boss, or colleague—who could benefit from it and who will not abuse the confidence. In my friend's words, that's "gabbing up." You've betrayed a confidence, but with a defined purpose and within a very small circle of people. You've controlled the leak. No harm, no foul.

It's a much more serious offense to share that information with people who don't matter to you or who have no need to know or who cannot be relied upon to keep it to themselves.

This is "gabbing down." It comes in many forms, nearly all of them variations on "I know something you don't know" (e.g., you want to impress someone that you are "in the know" or you feel you have to give some information in order to get something back). In essence, you are trafficking in gossip. There's no defined purpose to your little betrayal. No one benefits from it. Worst of all, you're not controlling the leak. When you don't know whom you're talking to, you may as well be talking to the world.

HOW TO PROTECT A SECRET

Secrets are like Pandora's Box. Once open, they can easily spiral out of control. Thus, taking precautions is a basic communication skill.

That's the point behind the phrase "gabbing up." I don't share secrets lightly. I share them only with people who have a long track record of being discreet. That's the definition of a "confidant" or "friend" in my book.

People have all sorts of verbal devices that help them stamp a piece of information as "classified" or "confidential." There's almost a grading system to the information. If they say, "This is top secret," that implies a certain level of confidentiality. If they say, "Before I tell you anything, you have to promise that it doesn't leave this room," that suggests a slightly more serious level of confidentiality.

My friend who coined the gabbing up and down distinction has his own method for grading secrets.

When he shares a semi-serious confidence, he always prefaces it by reminding the other party that the information is "embargoed." The implication here is that breaking the embargo might upset or harm the person who originally shared the secret with him.

More serious secrets are "double embargoed." The implication is that two people might be affected.

The most sensitive secrets are "triple embargoed," implying that any sort of breach would affect three people: the person who originally shared the secret; the person who broke the secret; and the person who broke the "triple embargo." The greatest damage, of course, would be to the reputation of the third individual in the chain. "After such a stern warning," says my friend, "I don't think I would ever trust that person again."

I'm not being naive when I knowingly and purposefully break a confidence. I only do so with people I trust absolutely. These people know implicitly—without the harsh warning—that the information is "triple embargoed." Experience has taught them as well as me that a thoughtless breach of the confidence will harm at least three parties.

TREAT THE UNVARNISHED TRUTH WITH GRATITUDE

A woman in our classical music division was considering representing a rather eccentric musician who wanted to establish a career as a conductor. She sat in on his orchestra rehearsals to see how he handled musicians. She went to several of his concerts to hear how he interpreted the classics and to gauge his rapport with a live audience. None of these forays made much of an impression on her, until one day the conductor invited her to a lecture he was giving on creative management to students at a business school. She was amazed at what she saw. Sitting at a piano, the conductor made some dazzling and amusing analogies between what composers and professional managers do. The students gave him a standing ovation.

In the end the woman concluded that representing this musician would not be a good use of her time, and she candidly told him why. "Face it," she said, "you'll never be Sir Georg Solti, because you're too strange and you're just not that good a musician."

She did add that he could have a lucrative career as an entertainer on the fringes of classical music and in front of business groups.

"Your future," she said, "is talking to amateurs—because the real professionals know you are nuts!"

Now, that last remark may seem gratuitously cruel. But in fact, it was priceless advice. In one neat sentence, she had given this man a career niche. She had turned him away from his fruitless pursuit of a major-league conducting career and steered him in a direction that capitalized on all his eccentricities.

I suspect a lot of people could use that sort of candor in assessing their careers. But the fact is, when it comes to their careers, most people don't invite candor. And even when they get it, they have trouble accepting it.

I don't know how many times people in our company have come to me, saying, "I don't think you're using me correctly. I really want to work in another area." Invariably, they want to move out of a job that they perceive as mundane into a job that seems more glamorous.

It falls on me to reshift their thinking, to candidly tell them that we have people in the company who are stronger in that area than they are, and that they could contribute more by staying where they are and perfecting their skills. Some accept my opinion. Others don't.

We once had an executive who had a lot of very desirable virtues. He was brilliant, well organized, and strong on follow-through. But he was rough on his subordinates. He second-guessed them and generally made their lives miserable. After a while, nearly all of them sought asylum in another part of our company or left us altogether. On several occasions I tried to show him that his harsh manner was costly to him and to the company. But he refused to believe me—or at least he refused to change.

In my experience, the most successful people are the ones who are the most brutally honest about their abilities. They don't delude themselves about their weaknesses. And they conduct frequent reality checks by inviting others to tell them how they're doing.

I've always liked the adage that "One of the best ways to measure people is to watch how they behave when you offer them something for free."

I think you can tell even more about a person by how they react to criticism.

Check yourself: How have you reacted in the past when someone you trust has offered you heartfelt but hard-to-swallow advice? You have several options.

There's *curiosity*. You try to corroborate the advice by seeking a second or third opinion.

There's *skepticism*. You file the critique in the back of your mind, perhaps to revisit it when you are more open to believing it.

There's *denial*. You conclude the advice is wrong.

But the most appropriate response is *gratitude*. When friends step out on a limb to tell you the unvarnished truth about yourself, you should embrace them, not leave them hanging out there alone.

CHAPTER 5

The Many Faces of "No"

HERE ARE FOUR THINGS I KNOW ABOUT THE WORD "NO":

- It is the second shortest word in the English language.

- It is the most definitive word in its meaning. That's why people say, "No means no." There's no other way to express it.

- It is the toughest word for people to say.

- It is even tougher for people to hear and understand.

That's the problem with "no." It is so terse and abrupt, so rude in its unambiguous negativity, that a lot of people can't deal with it. They don't know how to deliver it properly. They say "no" when they really mean maybe. They say "maybe" when they're really thinking no. They think "no" is confrontational so they gingerly circle around the word to avoid confrontation. With all this confusion surrounding the utterance of "no," is it any wonder that a lot of people have trouble understanding it?

I have always regarded "no" as the most important word in an executive's vocabulary. I have learned the hard way that failing to say "no" can lose you more money than saying "yes" can ever make you. When it comes to decision making, I do everything in my power to say no before I say yes. All this effort has taught me a few secrets about "no" that make it easier to say and easier for other people to swallow.

1. NO IS NOT A CONFRONTATION.

We use "no" in its most basic form to fend off other people who want us to do something we don't want to do. We have the choice of being polite or hostile in how we say no.

Some people use no as a form of aggression. To these people, saying no to someone is a power play, an opportunity to assert their superiority over that individual. They enjoy saying no, because it creates a confrontation they know they can win. Unfortunately, this approach doesn't wear well for very long. At some point, people stop dealing with you altogether.

Some years ago, a friend of mine in the entertainment business had the chance to represent a major performing artist. In checking him out, my friend found out that the artist was very difficult and had alienated a lot of people in his business. He was perceived as difficult because he would turn every artistic decision into a confrontation. "No, I won't work with that director," or "No, I don't like that set design." Part of this, I'm sure, was artistic integrity, but most of it was the petulant stirrings of a prima donna and bully. After years of listening to him say no, few people were willing to work with him. My friend politely declined the chance to represent him.

The irony is that I've known a lot of superstars, in sports and the performing arts, who are just as successful at fending people off and getting their own way. But they know how to make people feel good when they tell them no. They don't turn no into a confrontation. When they say no, they're sorry about it. "Gee, I wish I could help you, but the timing is bad for me. I'm afraid I'll have to say no." They make their point, but they take the sting out of no.

2. EVERY NO NEEDS AN EXPLANATION.

The most dangerous no is the one you don't explain. I'm sure we've all had the following conversation as either parent or child:

Child asks parent for permission to do something.

Parent says no.

Child asks why.

Parent offers a specific reason.

Child asks why again.

Parent elaborates on the explanation.

Child asks why again.

Parent explodes with the brilliant response, "Because I said so!"

There's a healthy venting process going on here. Between the initial "no" and the final desperate "because I said so," the child has squeezed out an explanation from the parent.

The child may not like the answer, but he knows the reasoning behind it.

That doesn't always happen in business. Not all bosses have the patience, time, or communication skills to lean back in their chair and illuminate the logic behind their definitive "no." But they should. Likewise, not all subordinates have the self-assurance to press their boss for a complete explanation. But they should.

3. SOMETIMES NO MEANS YES.

One of the dangers of not explaining "no" is that people don't believe you mean it. When you say "no," they think you mean maybe—which is an invitation for them to stick around until you say "yes." That's not the most sure-footed way to make decisions or manage people.

One of the pleasures of working with Arnold Palmer was his definitive delivery of a yes or no. If I presented him with an offer to play a golf exhibition in Cincinnati on a Tuesday in October and he wasn't inclined to do it, he wouldn't waffle. He'd say no and give me a legitimate reason, e.g., "I need the time to practice," or "I want to spend some time at home." And he wouldn't second guess himself once he made up his mind. That's a wonderful luxury in business. I'd much rather have a client tell me no right away (even if it means saying good-bye to a nice payday) than keep me twisting in the wind and holding off the customer on the off chance that he might say yes. A definitive no lets me move onto something else. A maybe freezes me into inaction.

Of course, it's nice that Arnold had me to play the "bad cop," telling everyone no. But that's another facet of no. If you're in a position where you frequently have to say no to people, it's not a bad idea to find someone to do it for you.

4. TAKE TIME TO SAY NO.

A police chief in Massachusetts once told me that she never had a problem going to her state's then-governor, Michael Dukakis, with a funding request, even though she knew there was no chance he would approve it.

The reason: "He would take his time before he turned you down. He would hear me out, let me make my speech, and then he would make his speech. He'd tell me how his hands were tied by the legislature, how there was only so much money to go around, and how he couldn't help me even if he wanted to. By the time he said no, I felt more sorry for him than me."

That may be the real secret to saying no. People won't be hurt if you dismiss their suggestions or requests, not if you give them a fair hearing and take your time explaining your side. The slow, measured no may not seem as decisive as the on-the-spot no, but it's easier for your people to accept—and that makes it more commanding.

NO NEWS IS BAD NEWS

I was in a staff meeting once when one of our senior managers asked an associate when we could expect a response to a proposal from one of our major corporate customers. It was an elaborate proposal, prepared at the customer's request, and we hadn't heard anything about it in weeks.

"We'll hear in a few days," said the associate.

Then, in a vain attempt to put a positive spin on the situation, he added, "At least they haven't turned it down. No news is good news."

The manager jumped all over the associate. "You're wrong," he said. "If they were interested in it, they would have told us by now. They either don't like it, or they have major doubts, or they don't have the guts to tell us no after making us jump through all these hoops, or they're stalling so we don't take the idea to someone else. But the truth is, no news is *bad* news."

It was a valid point. Silence from the other side is rarely a good sign. Common sense tells you that when good news is involved, people don't hesitate to deliver it. The act of saying, "Yes, I'll buy it," is a wholly positive experience. The people delivering the good news feel good about it; the people on the receiving end feel even better.

Conversely, when bad news is involved, it's only natural that people stall in delivering it. Saying "no" to someone is, by definition, a negative experience. It means you're rejecting them. It brands you as the source of someone else's disappointment or pain. It also can lead to confrontation, and most people prefer to avoid confrontation. No wonder people would rather tell someone nothing than tell them "no."

The irony is that if people delivered or demanded bad news as openly and eagerly as they delivered or demanded good news, the world would be a better place and the workplace far more efficient. All sorts of misunderstandings and conflicts could be avoided.

In my experience, this is true whether you're saying no or hearing it. In both cases, you're far better off dealing with it quickly rather than slowly, aggressively rather than passively, frontally rather than obliquely.

It helps if you first acknowledge two of the biggest reasons that people are less eager to say "no" than "yes."

The biggest reason, I suspect, is that they're afraid to appear confrontational.

For example, my wife Betsy is the nicest person I know. It is not in her nature to say "no" to people if she thinks that it will offend them or hurt their feelings. This quality is slightly complicated by the fact that she has been a professional tennis player for twenty years and is a broadcaster on ESPN and ABC. In other words, she's widely traveled and knows a lot of people in tennis. Knowing a wide net of people tends to increase the number of favors asked of you.

Let's say a civic group asks her to give a talk to a high school audience or conduct a tennis clinic (a frequent request). If she can fit it into her schedule, she will gladly say yes. (Nothing wrong with that.) If there's a fifty-fifty chance that she can make it happen, she will say so but give considerably more than a fifty-fifty effort to deliver. (Again, nothing wrong with that sort of "definite maybe.")

The trouble starts when she knows that she almost certainly can't make the date. Rather than resolve the situation with a definitive "no," she'll delay a decision on the chance that a change in her schedule might free her up for the event. That desire to please is admirable, but in reality, it often damages rather than improves the situation. Waiting for Betsy,

93

the other party holds off on asking their second choice or, worse, assumes that by not saying "no" my wife has more or less said "yes." When Betsy ultimately can't make the date, the other side is both disappointed and farther behind than when they started. It doesn't matter that Betsy is doing them a favor. A big part of their disappointment is laid at her feet. Betsy would have been better off if she had confronted the situation immediately. The other side would have been happier too.

Unresolved gray areas in a situation are the other big reason people hesitate delivering bad news. They would rather leave the gray areas gray, especially if doing so works to their advantage.

A businesswoman I know who runs a small consulting firm gave me a vivid reminder that "no news is bad news." She had been asked by her biggest account to give a speech at the company's annual convention. For doing so, she would receive her usual fee of $4,000 a day. There was no dispute over the day rate. The client was accustomed to paying for the time she spent with company executives, including travel time. But preparing a one-hour speech takes time, too. She told her contact at the company, the vice president of corporate communications, that a half-day fee of $2,000 would be fair. The VP let this additional fee go unremarked. He neither challenged it nor agreed to it. He let it hang there.

After the speech, which was a big success, she invoiced the client $6,000—$4,000 for her day rate and $2,000 for "preparation." A $4,000 check arrived promptly, but the $2,000 charge went unpaid. When she called the VP about this oversight, he pleaded ignorance and said, "Let me look into it."

Nothing happened. She called again, only to get the same lame excuse. This went on for weeks.

She eventually resolved the matter by going over the VP's head and appealing to the company's CEO. The CEO paid the bill immediately (which says a lot about why he's the CEO and the VP is not).

But this woman learned a larger lesson about the danger of gray areas in a business relationship.

"My first mistake," she later told me, "was not getting that $2,000 on the record the first time I mentioned it. I should have forced the VP to agree to it verbally and then confirmed it in writing. In that sense, I'm as much to blame as he is. My second mistake was not realizing that he was stonewalling me, hoping I'd drop the $2,000. I should have known that the first time he wouldn't say 'yes' to my invoice, he was really telling me 'no.' "

There are countless parallel situations in business where gray areas turn into black holes because no one has the gumption to confront them right away.

A negotiation can go smoothly on all fronts, but if there is one thorny issue that the other side regularly skirts, you can be sure that this is the deal point that will eventually get everyone shouting at each other and possibly kill the deal.

Likewise with a sale that has gone well past the contract stage. If vague promises (anything from next-day delivery to free technical support to a 5 percent discount for immediate payment) have been made along the way—without explicit confirmation—you can be sure that the buyer will attach more value to these promises and remember them more clearly than will the seller.

Remember, when the person you're dealing with—whether it's a customer, vendor, boss, or colleague—repeatedly refuses to address an issue, there's only one way to interpret the silence. It means bad news for all concerned.

ARE YOU HEARING "YES" WHEN THEY REALLY MEAN "NO"?

I tend to admire people who can say "No" and mean it, even if I'm on the receiving end of that bad news—because a firm "No" at least tells me where I stand. I would much rather hear a definitive "No" that lets me move on to other things than a "maybe" that keeps me twisting in the wind.

Unfortunately, not everyone is good at saying no. It is, by definition, a negative gesture. At the very least, it means you will disappoint someone who wants something from you.

So people develop ways to mean no without actually saying it. They waffle. They say "I'll get back to you" or "Let me think about that." Anything to buy time so that you—and your problem—will go away.

In business, there are two types of people who regularly get to tell you no: Your customers and your colleagues. Ironically, it's your colleagues you have to worry about.

Customers, as a general rule, don't have a problem saying no. It's their job (and they know you expect it sometimes).

Colleagues, on the other hand, are often less than candid. After all, they have to see you every day. You're usually not asking them for something as tangible as money, nor are you offering a product or service in exchange. What you most often require from your colleagues is their help and their time. These are vague requests. And so they vaguely tell you no. Here are four ways your coworkers can keep you hanging on.

1. BENIGN NEGLECT

In it's most common form, benign neglect is the worker who says, "Yes, I'll help you," and then does nothing. He makes promises with no intention of delivering them, secure in the knowledge that the longer he makes you wait for his help, the less likely you will need him. His goal is to appear cooperative without actually being so.

The key to converting this veiled no into a yes is to start out with easy tasks and very short deadlines. If you make easy requests, your colleagues are more likely to do them. If you tell them you need it the next day, you'll know their true answer within twenty-four hours.

2. PLEADING IGNORANCE

This is the colleague who evades your request not by saying, "I don't want to help you," but rather "I don't know how." He would rather look stupid than help you look smart. Don't bother trying to educate him or bring him up to speed. You'd be wasting your time.

3. PLEADING OMNISCIENCE

This is the opposite of pleading ignorance. Rather than saying "I don't know how," the colleague says, "I need to know more." And so he peppers you with questions, knowing that eventually you won't have an answer, at which point he can excuse himself and return to his job while you wander back to the drawing board to rethink your request.

4. APPEALING TO A HIGHER AUTHORITY

This is the colleague who responds to your request by saying, "Let me check with my boss." This is saying no by changing the jurisdiction. The colleague doesn't have to refuse; he lets a third party—namely the boss—do it for him. Don't bother waiting for him to get back to you.

I don't mean to suggest that organizations are infested with devious sharpies who can't look you in the eye or shoot straight. In fact, the opposite is true. Most people are cooperative by nature—so cooperative that they try to be helpful even when it's beyond their powers to do so. Recognize the true signals your colleagues are sending you and they'll rarely disappoint you. You'll save yourself a career's worth of frustration and rarely have to make up for lost time.

CHAPTER 6

Dealing One-on-One

NINE WAYS TO WIN AN ARGUMENT

We all know people who love to argue. Whether they are right or wrong (and especially if they're wrong), they somehow manage to get their way with us through sheer will, fervor, or loudness.

Don't delude yourself. Winning arguments is not always a matter of being relentless or loud. The people who consistently win arguments when the merits are a toss-up tend to employ some very clever stratagems designed to put their opponents at a disadvantage. If you find yourself regularly losing arguments that you should be winning, here are nine stratagems that can improve your track record. If nothing else, be aware the next time these stratagems or ruses are being employed against you.

1. REPHRASE THE PREMISE.

There's no easier way to take control of a debate than to rephrase your opponent's premise in language that is most favorable to you. You can usually tell your opponent is adopting this approach if he responds to you by saying, "You mean to tell me . . ." and then proceeds to misstate or exaggerate everything you've said. Your response should always be corrective: "That's not what I said at all."

2. CATEGORIZE THE ARGUMENT.

By placing your opponent's argument into a category, preferably one that is unfashionable or disreputable, you automatically infect his argument with all the negatives associated with that category. For example, if you disagree with a subordinate who suggests that everyone in the company should participate equally in a profit-sharing program, you refute him by saying, "That's communism."

Bosses often use a variation on this technique when subordinates challenge their authority by trying to put an issue to a popular vote. A clever boss can prevent a vote by simply announcing, "This is not a democracy."

3. LIKEN THE CONCEPT TO SOMEONE ELSE'S FAILURE.

It is relatively easy to knock a new idea by suggesting that (a) it is not new at all, and (b) that it was a fiasco in its previous incarnation. For example, if you have a new marketing idea for

Coca-Cola, your opponent may try to dismiss you by responding, "Pepsi tried that five years ago and failed."

The good news is that it is also relatively easy to refute this stratagem—by pointing out that changes in the marketplace over those five years make it an even better idea today.

4. ASK FOR PROOF.

When they are not trying to bully their way through an argument, the most dazzling debaters often try to bluff. If you know they are misstating facts in order to strengthen their conclusion, don't let them get away with it.

If your opponent says, "In 1991 we had a 30 percent increase in expenses in the XYZ division," and you suspect (but do not know) that the figure is inflated to suit his purposes, ask him to prove it. There is no discourtesy in challenging him. If he is right, he has gained nothing. If he is wrong or cannot support his statement, you have cast doubt on everything else he may say.

5. AGREE IN PRINCIPLE, BUT DEBATE THE SPECIFICS.

People tend to hear what they want to hear in any debate. Thus, if you tell your opponent, "I agree with you in principle," it is quite possible that all he hears is that you agree with him. He doesn't pay as close attention as you state your objections or gently take apart his argument point by point.

Agreeing in principle is also a popular stalling tactic. Quite often, when people agree in principle, they never get around to resolving the specifics of an argument. The winner in that case is the party who has more to gain by leaving the matter unresolved. For example, if you ask your boss for a significant budget increase for your department, he may agree in principle. You may leave his office elated. But if you never resolve the details—that is, if you never get him to commit to a specific number—you have won nothing.

6. INTERRUPT.

This is a shameless but underappreciated stratagem—because most people are polite and tend to give their opponent a fair opportunity to state his case. But interrupting is a great way to distract your opponent, particularly if you know his case is much stronger than yours.

If you think interrupting is a dirty trick, note how often in your next argument a strong opponent will not give you a chance to finish a sentence or make a point. It's more popular than you think.

7. ADMIT NOTHING.

In almost all arguments, the opposing sides agree on certain base issues. Upon these jointly held beliefs, the argument then proceeds. However, a good debater will challenge even these base issues. He admits nothing.

Let's say you open a discussion by saying, "We all agree that we have to cut capital spending by 25 percent. The question is where do we cut." A strong opponent might reject that initial premise: "I don't agree. If everyone else is cutting, we should be spending even more." In effect, he has forced the debate in another direction. He may not win the argument. But he has distracted everyone else; you may never get around to making the necessary spending cuts.

8. QUESTION THEIR MOTIVES.

Your opponent may have perfectly legitimate reasons for taking a certain position, but by casting doubt on his motives you can diminish the strength of his reasoning.

For example, your chief rival suggests moving the New York office to New Jersey, where office space is cheaper and taxes are lower. If you oppose the move, you may ask your rival, "Are you sure you don't want to move the office there because you live in a neighboring town and commuting is more convenient for you?" Demonstrate that self-interest is your rival's prime motivation for suggesting the move and everyone may ignore cheaper office space and lower taxes.

9. APPEAL TO OTHERS IN THE ROOM.

This is a personal favorite, particularly if I anticipate a confrontation in a public forum. At some point during a dispute, I will turn to an associate and say, "Well, let's hear what Joe has to say on the subject." By injecting a third party into the debate I not only have depersonalized the dispute (it's no longer a duel between two egos) but I have strengthened my case by demonstrating that other people support it.

It is essential that you know who your allies are beforehand and advisable that they know what you are doing.

THE BOSS'S JOKES ARE ALWAYS FUNNY (EVEN WHEN THEY AREN'T)

I try to be an acute observer of the power games people play at all levels of business, the finesse moves they employ to one-up their adversaries, rivals, and peers. But a longtime friend opened my eyes to a totally new power indicator.

This gentleman is a very successful entrepreneur in the entertainment business. Outside his industry, he is not a household name—which is how he prefers it. But his impact on American culture is considerable. He is wealthy and has been his own boss for years, which suggests that he is accustomed to (and aware of) the kind of deference normally reserved for tycoons, heads of state, and legends.

His greatest skill, perhaps, is his ability to spot and develop talent.

He told me about his early years when he had just discovered a young performer. He devoted a huge amount of time to managing and counseling this artist and discussing his career with both him and his family. The performer was not unappreciative. In fact, he was in awe of my friend and extremely solicitous of everything he said. He followed my friend's suggestions, met with him whenever he wanted to, listened to his war stories, and laughed at his jokes at meetings or over dinner.

Years passed, during which this particular performer became a very big star.

Not long ago my friend and his wife had occasion to spend a lot of time socially with this superstar. Over the course of several dinners together they couldn't help noticing how the superstar assumed control of conversation at the table with an incessant stream of show business anecdotes and banter.

The strange part was that my friend and his wife felt compelled to laugh at these tales, even though they weren't particularly funny.

"It's an interesting line you cross," he said, "when you find yourself with someone who used to laugh at your jokes—and now you have to laugh at theirs."

I mention this because I think there are unspoken but clear power lines drawn in almost every business or social relationship. And you ignore them at your own peril.

I sensed this years ago when I started out with Arnold Palmer and Gary Player. If Arnold or Gary were present, whether it was a business meeting, on the golf course, or at a cocktail party, they were the stars and I was a supporting player. (Part of this at the time was a function of my relative youth and their unquestioned celebrity as champion athletes. But things haven't changed all that much in the ensuing years, even though I'm no longer a rookie and have a few triumphs of my own. I still defer to the client. That's part of the job.)

Conversely, as a CEO, I sense the tables may have turned when it comes to power and my subordinates. There's probably some truth in the fact that our employees feel that they have to laugh at my jokes (even when they're not funny). That same superior-to-subordinate dynamic applies to everyone, all the way down the chain of command.

How can you put this interpersonal dynamic to use in business?

For one thing, you should recognize that if you're in a dominant position in a business relationship or situation, quite often you're expected to carry the conversational ball.

It's a responsibility that comes with the territory. If you or your subordinates fail to recognize that, disasters can happen.

A few years ago, I took along three associates on a sales call to meet the chairman of a company we were eager to do business with. Perhaps the meeting should have been a one-on-one between me and the chairman. But we had met privately before and I wanted to expose him to some of the experts at our company. Two of the associates were twenty-year veterans of our company and knew how I operated in such meetings. The third fellow was brand new and had never been in such a situation with me.

It was a very frustrating sales call. The new associate took it upon himself to carry the conversational ball. This wasn't all bad. He knows his subject better than I do and articulates it well. But he went on forever. I tried to make eye contact with him, hoping he would let the chairman say something or ask questions, but every time there was a silence he would burst in with another oration. I've always thought that some of the most key moments in a negotiation occur when you let the other side speak and I could see this advantage slipping from my grasp.

It was aggravating because I had let him carry the ball but (to continue the football analogy) he wasn't letting me call the plays.

Admittedly, it was my fault. I had taken for granted that he understood the dynamic of a sales call with the boss.

If I'm the boss in a room with three associates, it should be obvious that I'm the person responsible for making the meeting work, for making the sale happen or not, and for making an impression that's good rather than bad. I should be calling the plays. But he was new and didn't know our playbook.

In hindsight, I should have had a practice session. Before the meeting, I should have told him, "Don't say anything until I ask you to. If somebody asks you a direct question, answer it, of course. But be brief and turn the dialogue back to me. When it's your turn, I'll cue you by asking, 'Joe, what do you think?' or 'Joe may have some interesting things to say about this.' "

As I say, most of us have a good instinct for the lines of power in a meeting or negotiation. We know when to be deferential and when we should be deferred to. We display this in dozens of little ways—from how we seat ourselves at a conference table, to who opens the meeting, to how long we talk, to who we can interrupt and who we can't. Acknowledging these power lines will never hurt you. Ignoring them will never help.

GETTING A CLEARER MESSAGE
FROM BODY LANGUAGE

When it comes to body language, I try to remind myself to keep my own personal body language to a minimum in sales and negotiating situations. A neutral demeanor is still the best way to prevent the other side from knowing what you're really thinking.

My big problem with body language has always been its imprecision of meaning. When the prospect starts tapping his fingers during your sales pitch, it may mean he's not interested. But you can never be sure. It could be nothing more than a nervous habit or someone playing out a private drumbeat.

107

I have also met with people who, at crucial points in a negotiation when they intend to get serious, will unknowingly "lean into" the conversation, or unconsciously push aside their papers to give me their undivided attention. Yet just as often, I have seen people at similar points lean back in their chair and strike a relaxed pose.

Another problem is that, although body language is supposed to be unconscious, some people consciously use it for effect—and get it all wrong!

Public speakers, for example, will raise their voice to get their audience's attention, even though whispering might be more effective (and less annoying). Young executives will talk rapidly and make shotgun decisions to appear more authoritative, even though a less frenzied pace is usually more impressive.

I also have a problem with the sequence people use to interpret body language. For most people, the sequence goes like this: First, they spot a nonverbal cue (e.g., the prospect leans forward in his chair). Then they attach a meaning to it (the prospect's interest has been piqued). The problem here is that you can spend so much mental energy seeking out these indirect signals and decoding their messages that you miss what people are actually saying to you.

I prefer to reverse this sequence. First I construct a mental checklist of crucial messages that I want the other side to send out during our discussion. Then I look for nonverbal cues to support it.

I'm not sure this meaning first, signal second system works for everyone, but it certainly works for people in sales situations. The vital messages circulating in the room during a sales call or negotiation are universal and unyielding. Everyone in the room is curious about the same things.

- Is the other side interested?

- Are they telling the truth?

- Do they like me?

- Do they have the budget?

- Do they have the authority to make a decision?

- Are they ready to close?

Body language alone won't provide answers to all these questions. For example, in all my years of selling I still haven't found a subtle or indirect way to determine if the other side can afford my price. There's no body language that indicates the size of someone's budget. To find that out, I'm still better off asking directly, "Do you have the budget for this?"

Where body language is helpful, though, is precisely in the areas where (a) people cannot ask direct questions, and (b) even if they could, the other side might not answer them. Consider the following three messages.

1. WHO'S GOT THE POWER?

You don't usually need body language to determine who has power in a meeting. If the other side's CEO is in the room, the answer is obvious. What you don't know, however, and can't always determine from job titles, is who the CEO's favorites are and whom you will be dealing with after the CEO has left the room. In other words, who's second in command?

I look for cues that a person is comfortable in the CEO's presence. In many companies, the boss has a chilling, intimidating effect on employees. They don't behave normally around the boss. They're stiff. They're overalert. They're too quick to laugh at the boss's jokes.

I look for the opposite in people. People with power are comfortable around other powerful people. They're relaxed. They make themselves comfortable (but not to the point that they slouch in their seats; people with power maintain a certain amount of dignity and professional bearing). They sit directly in the CEO's sight line, often on the far side of the table, rather than next to the CEO. They don't bring a legal pad to take notes.

One of the more telling power signs: Which people feel free to interrupt or contradict the CEO? An even more telling sign: Which people get away with it with the CEO?

2. WHO'S TELLING THE TRUTH?

There's one overwhelming reason people take an interest in body language: so they can tell when someone is lying. They look for the obvious mannerisms: averting the eyes, rapid blinking, covering the mouth to speak, shrugging shoulders, looking down, wetting the lips, swallowing repeatedly, clearing the throat, rubbing the back of the neck, or scratching the head while speaking.

Perhaps I'm too cynical, but with people I don't know well, I always assume they are shading the truth in our discussion. I don't mean that the other side is proactively lying or making up numbers. But they may be omitting key facts that tilt the dialogue in their favor.

As a result, I'm alert to those rare moments when I know I'm getting the unvarnished truth.

I was once sitting at a table at a wedding reception with an old friend and his wife. I hadn't seen the man in years and casually asked how his business was doing. His answer was cheery and upbeat. Ten minutes later I heard his wife, a few seats away, paint a decidedly different picture to another woman at our table. The wife said the business was failing, they had to borrow money from her parents, and so on.

At that moment, if I had any doubts about whether husband or wife was telling the truth, the man's body language erased all doubt. As his wife spoke, I could see him tense up and his eyes widen.

These clues were revealing but not conclusive. But when he stood up, walked around the table, pulled up a chair next to his wife, and put his arm around her—a courtly equivalent of putting his hand over her mouth—I knew she was telling the truth.

I've noticed the same response in business meetings when someone from the other side starts giving away more information than his or her bosses think I should know.

Real numbers—sales figures, profit margins, how much someone got paid—are always the toughest details to extract from the other side. So whenever I hear someone spouting out actual numbers in a meeting I not only note the numbers, but I look at the other people across the table. Do they have a panicked look in their eyes? Are they clearing their throats or doing something with their hands to catch their talkative colleague's attention? Do they lean imperceptibly toward the colleague, as if they're fighting to be the first to interrupt? If so, I know I'm hearing the truth.

3. IT'S TIME TO CLOSE THE DEAL.

The best way to close a deal, of course, is to ask for the order directly. Body language, however, can give you invaluable timing cues.

For one thing, you never want to ask for the order too soon, before the prospect is fully convinced that he needs your product or service. In my experience, crossed arms over the chest are the clearest sign that a prospect remains unpersuaded by your pitch. Crossed arms are the ultimate defensive gesture. They're code for all sorts of statements, from "Show me" to "I'm skeptical" to "I need to know much more than you're telling me." The one thing they don't say is, "I'm ready to buy." If the prospect is sitting in front of you with crossed arms (or weaker variations such as clasped hands or crossed legs), that's not the time to ask for the order.

The good news here, of course, is that sometimes the prospect shifts out of a defensive posture. The shift can signal a change in attitude.

In my experience, when a prospect uncrosses his arms or unclasps his hands, it either means the meeting is over or I should prepare to ask for the order. At those moments, I study the prospective client's eyes and hands. If the eyes are looking directly at me, that's a good sign. It means I've made a connection. As for the hands, if the prospect is rubbing them (an incredibly crude but revealing sign of satisfaction and anticipation), it means I've made a sale.

RESIST HASTY CONCLUSIONS WITH BODY LANGUAGE

It's not that I don't think there's a message behind body language. There usually is. But you have to resist hasty conclusions and conventional interpretations. They can lead you totally astray.

John Macklin, the head of our investment arm in Cleveland, told me about a series of meetings where body language was a critical—but ultimately misleading—factor. One of Macklin's financial management clients, a successful CEO of a European conglomerate, had asked Macklin to find him a banker to handle the financing of a personal investment. After screening a few choices, Macklin set up a meeting between his favorite banker and this CEO. Unfortunately, the banker didn't distinguish himself in the first meeting. His presentation about the bank's capabilities was not well prepared and his financing ideas were banal. At least that's how it appeared to Macklin.

Yet when he looked over at the CEO, the man was rigid in rapt attention. He asked sharp questions and seemed to be satisfied with the answers. At first, this surprised Macklin. He had always considered the CEO to be financially sophisticated and a shrewd judge of people. Why was he enthralled with this less-than-stellar banker? Macklin rationalized that the CEO was being polite and going through the motions until the meeting was over.

A few weeks later, Macklin got another surprise. The CEO wanted a second meeting with the banker. Again, Macklin set it up. Again, the banker was less than brilliant. Again, the CEO appeared polite, inquisitive, and deferential. A few times this deference came at Macklin's expense, with the CEO reminding Macklin about previous financial schemes that had gone awry and pointedly asking the banker if he would have done the same thing.

This pattern of pleasant meetings between the CEO and the banker was repeated several more times during the year. For his part, Macklin was confused. The discussions were going nowhere, yet everything in the CEO's behavior and body language suggested that he was keenly interested. Macklin was also stung by the harsh treatment he was getting from the CEO in these meetings.

Then one day, the CEO called Macklin and asked him, "John, this banker isn't very impressive, is he?"

"No, he's not," replied Macklin.

"He hasn't really come up with any ideas we can use, has he?"

"No, he hasn't," replied Macklin.

"We really should be talking to other banks, shouldn't we?"

"Yes, we should," said Macklin. "I wasn't aware you realized that. It was my impression that you liked him. You don't suffer fools gladly. Why did you want to meet with him so often and why were you so polite?"

"My mother taught me that good manners is the best defense mechanism in strange environments or when you're dealing with strangers. That way, no one can get too close to you and figure out what you're thinking. Being polite was the best way to get a lot of information from the banker."

"That's fine," said Macklin, "but that doesn't explain some of your harsh comments about me."

"That's easy," said the CEO. "I can pick on you because you're like family to me. I don't need a defense mechanism with you."

That's the risk of putting too much faith in body language. The CEO consciously adopted a demeanor and body language that served his purposes. But Macklin (and perhaps the banker as well) misread the message.

That doesn't mean we should completely mistrust body language or discount the value of our impressions. But any insight becomes a little more reliable when it's folded in with other subtle indicators.

I pay a lot of attention to the factor of time and how it affects our perception of a situation or a message.

For example, I've noticed that people tend to equate a project's significance with how much of their time it requires or how much time other people devote to it, even though quite often the opposite is the case.

If you attend a speech scheduled to last sixty minutes and the speaker only talks for thirty minutes, you very likely will feel cheated. Even if the speaker has covered the material succinctly and spared you thirty minutes of hot air, you will feel short-changed. A topic vital to you has somehow been diminished.

The same thing happens when people go into a one-hour meeting with the boss and it ends on a positive note in fifteen minutes. No matter how encouraging the boss's verbal statements and body language, some people take their curtailed stay as a sign that they and their ideas are less important. Their preconception about time has forced them to misread the clues and the situation completely.

I tend to go the other way. In my mind, if a meeting lasts shorter than scheduled or a problem resolves itself quickly, I always take that as a good sign, because it invariably is.

I made a sales call on a London managing director not long ago, ostensibly to pitch a golf idea. That was the defined purpose of the meeting. However, the moment I entered the M.D.'s office, I was confronted with a dazzling array of stereo equipment and two massive speakers in the center of the room. The M.D. obviously liked music, and his eccentric office begged for comment. So I mentioned that our company was heavily involved in classical music. He was unaware of that but instantly lit up and leaned toward me to hear more. I proceeded to describe a concert series we were developing.

He interrupted me, saying, "Send me the proposal on that." Then with a sweep of his hands to indicate he was pushing that topic aside, he said, "Now, let's talk about golf."

Some people might interpret the M.D.'s sweeping gesture to be dismissive. If they coupled that with the brevity of the discussion, they might assume that the M.D. wasn't interested in music. But in truth, it was a positive sign. In the end, our music discussion lasted no more than five minutes and our golf talk took an hour, and yet the M.D. bought into the music project and we haven't talked about golf since.

EVEN THE BEST CLUES TAKE TIME TO APPRECIATE

In a speech to a group of human resources professionals, I described some of the important insights you can pick up about people by aggressively observing their behavior on the golf course, the tennis court, what they order in restaurants, etc. A questioner from the audience thanked me for my remarks but wondered why I didn't talk about reading people in straight business situations. He said, "I would think that how people behave in business situations provides the truest insight into their character. Don't you agree?"

Not completely. The reason I think insights from the golf course or tennis court are important is precisely because they take place outside of the normal business routine, on weekends or in relaxed venues, where people let down their guard and, consciously or not, let the more interesting elements of their true character come out. That's less likely to occur in "straight business situations" when everyone is wearing their "game face" and studiously working to make the best impression.

The larger point: People clues can be found anywhere anytime, but the social and recreational fringes of business are a particularly rich (and underappreciated) source of insights.

The biggest problem I have with trying to gauge people in strictly business situations is that many clues are misleading or impossible to interpret. I know one extremely successful European conglomerateur who, five minutes into every meeting, pulls out an elaborate chain of silver worry beads and plays with them. If I didn't know him better, I might conclude that he was nervous or superstitious. If I wanted to overthink the situation, I might take special note of the subject we are discussing the moment he pulls out the beads—as if that were a valid indicator of the subject's importance to him. But the years have taught me that the beads indicate nothing—except perhaps that he is mildly eccentric. They are certainly not a sign of weakness or vulnerability.

The best way to pick up clues is to have a clear idea of what you're looking for. Before most meetings, I make a mental checklist of reasonable expectations. For example, if I'm calling on someone at their office, I can reasonably expect them to be cordial, to be punctual, and to hold all phone calls during our meeting. If they fail to meet one or more of these minimum requirements, that tells me something about them or, at least, about their attitude toward me.

Not long ago, two associates and I drove from New York to Pennsylvania for a noon meeting with a computer software company interested in developing a software product around one of our clients. Since we had been on the road for three hours and arrived at twelve o'clock sharp, it was not unreasonable for us to expect our hosts to serve us lunch. As we entered the building, I turned to my associates and said, "Let's see how buttoned-up these people are. Do you think they've thought about lunch for us." It turns out they didn't. They gave us a tour of the facility and hauled us straight into their conference room, never asking if we were hungry. I remember thinking then that this oversight was a bad omen. No matter how good the company's products were, the people would overlook some of the "real world" details in marketing them.

In hindsight, that's what happened. They made a great product with our client, but had no idea how to sell it.

Of course, it's dangerous to pigeonhole people on first meeting. The clues they send out take time to appreciate.

A few years ago I had back-to-back meetings in a midwestern city with two nationally prominent entrepreneurs. Each of these men were powerful forces in their sports-crazy community and I thought it would be worthwhile to meet them and tell them about our company.

The first meeting was with a banking tycoon who could not have been more hospitable. He knew all about me and our company. He said he had been eager to meet me for years. He literally bathed me in the warm glow of his respect and admiration. I left his ornate wood-paneled chambers thinking, "That was a great meeting."

I then went across town to meet Tycoon No. 2 who could not have been less hospitable. He knew nothing about me or our company. He hadn't bothered to read the material I had sent him. He took at least five calls from his stockbroker during our discussion. It seemed all he wanted from me was some free marketing ideas for one of his underachieving divisions. He had no interest in charming or impressing me or making me feel comfortable. As I left his office, his subordinate who had brought us together actually apologized for his boss's rudeness.

I mention this as a caveat about reading people too quickly. Over the years we've done a lot of business with Tycoon No. 2 and absolutely nothing with the banker. And yet the day of our first meetings, I would have bet the opposite would be true. In hindsight, I think the banking tycoon was so nice because he knew no business would transpire between us; he treated my visit as a social call. On the other hand, I can

119

see now that Tycoon No. 2's no-nonsense style was a positive signal. That's the way he does business with everyone. In that sense, his rudeness was merely the opening move in his negotiating strategy.

That's the tricky part about insights. You can't rely on one clue. You have to accumulate clues constantly. You have to analyze them and play them against each other. And be sufficiently open-minded to adjust their meaning. Only then can you pick up insights that will give you an edge.

WHEN IT'S NOBODY'S BUSINESS BUT YOUR OWN

We used to have an executive in our company who was an incorrigible snoop. He had an insatiable need to know what everyone else in the company was doing—what project they were working on, with whom they were meeting, where they were traveling to. He wasn't sneaky about it. In fact, he was almost charmingly open when he pried.

One of his favorite tactics was to ask a senior executive's secretary about her boss's whereabouts. He would always phrase the question to imply that he already knew where the executive was: "Joe's in Atlanta today, isn't he?"

The secretary would correct him: "No, he's in Dallas for the week."

"Really!" this snoop would reply. "What's he doing there?"

And then the secretary would proceed to fill him on everything her boss was up to.

120

I have no idea what he did with all the "intelligence" he gathered this way, but he was amazingly persistent and democratic with this approach. He would pry into anyone's affairs—subordinates, colleagues, senior executives, even assistants on my staff. Even more amazing was how long it took people in our company to figure him out. For a number of years, he snooped unchallenged. Very few people had the savvy or the gumption to tell him, "That's none of your business."

I've always thought that some of the most awkward moments in business occur because people can't say, "It's none of your business." I'm sure we all know people who are naturally curious by nature. (Perhaps we number ourselves among this group.) But even the most curious people tend to know their place. They know what's appropriate and what's not. They know the difference between innocent curiosity and outright rudeness or invasion of privacy—and they usually don't go over the line.

For example, the snoop at our company was engaged in relatively harmless curiosity rather than corporate espionage. As I say, I don't know what he did with all the ephemera he gathered and I've never detected any damage to us as a result of his prying. But I suspect if he started asking some very detailed questions in quasi-confidential areas, most of our people would have cut him off immediately or, at least, started to suspect his motives.

Unfortunately, the world doesn't make it easy for us to gauge when someone's curiosity is appropriate and when it's not. There are gray areas in even the most sensitive discussions that can cause trouble or make us look bad—and not all of us have the wisdom or savvy to appreciate that.

As a general rule, there are two topics for which you should always have the phrase, "None of your business," on the tip of your tongue: *Someone else's money* and *your personal life.* Of all the topics that are nobody's business, these would seem to be the most obvious. But I am astonished at how aggressively people pry into these areas, how much people reveal on these subjects, and how few of us fully appreciate the consequences of doing so.

Consider the subject of money. All of us know that certain types of money discussions are taboo. In an era when people will gladly tell you how much they paid for their house or their jewelry, we still know that another person's salary is none of our business. Even with our best friend or our sister, we don't pry. But there are gray areas that confuse us, even on the subject of compensation.

Not long ago, one of our literary clients called up his agent in our New York office with an innocent-sounding request. We had just negotiated a fee for this writer to write the text of an illustrated book. For the work that needed to be done, the fee the publisher offered was fair and the writer agreed to it. As the writer began working on the book, however, he started having second thoughts about the illustrator's contribution to the project. So he called our office and asked us to find out what the illustrator was being paid. He didn't feel it was right if he was earning less than the illustrator. I suppose you could argue that this wasn't a totally inappropriate request. As agents, we want to get the best deal for our clients. But in another sense, the request was outrageous. In effect, our client was prying into the illustrator's paycheck.

The fact that the request involved someone else's money should have put our agent on red alert. The agent should have told the client, "You've accepted the fee. What the illustrator gets is none of your business." But our agent didn't do that. Acceding to the client's request, she called the publisher who, in so many words, told her, "Butt out!"

I can't help thinking that everyone would have come out smelling better if our agent had told the client, "It's none of your business." The client would not have looked like a whiner and meddler. The agent would not have gone on a fool's errand. And the publisher would have been spared an awkward confrontation.

Your personal life is another area that theoretically is nobody's business. Yet a lot of people allow the line between their professional and personal affairs to get blurred. Their inability to tell people to mind their own business can create unforeseen problems.

I can see how this happens in a normal working environment where bosses and subordinates are working eight-hour days together. Over time, as you develop a warm, friendly relationship with people at work, it's understandable when they become curious about some aspects of your personal life. They may know where you vacation with your family, whom you're dating, or what you do on the weekends. In my opinion, that's precisely the sort of information that's nobody's business—because you never know what your associates will do with that seemingly trivial information.

A few years ago I met with the CEO of another company and two of his senior staffers. One of the staffers wasn't as well informed as he should have been on one of the topics under discussion. The CEO snapped at him, "Maybe you'd know more if you didn't spend your evenings on the phone to your girlfriend in Chicago."

I was taken aback by the CEO's remark, not merely because of its crudity but because of the betrayal it implied. The staff person obviously trusted the CEO; at least he regarded him as enough of a friend to confide some details of his personal life. But the CEO abused that trust when he used that information to berate his subordinate in front of me. The normal boss-subordinate relationship was weakened by the fact that the two men were also friends. I can't help thinking that both men would have been better off if they had kept personal details out of their professional relationship, if at least one of them had regarded this information as nobody else's business.

PEOPLE WHO KNOW IT ALL DON'T ASK QUESTIONS. THEY ASK ANSWERS

I'm a big believer in saying "I don't know." It's one of the most effective ways to get rather than give information. It's also great for cutting off discussions that are going nowhere. And its meaning is never ambiguous. No one has ever created a misunderstanding by saying, "I don't know."

Today, when I presumably know more than I did twenty-five years ago, I find myself using the phrase more than ever. I even say "I don't know" when I *do* know—to find out how much the other person really knows. This self-effacing approach, this willingness to appear ignorant, is considerably more effective than pretending to be a know-it-all.

In my mind, know-it-alls are dangerous. They torture their subordinates, irritate their colleagues, and create havoc among their customers and clients. No matter how well they speak of themselves, their manner rarely speaks well for your company.

One telltale sign of a know-it-all is how he phrases his questions.

Know-it-alls don't ask questions. They ask answers— questions with the answer built in.

Rather than ask, "When did you buy your house?" the know-it-all says, "You bought your house two years ago, didn't you?"

The former sounds like an innocent question. The latter sounds like an accusation.

I could shrug all this off as one of the minor irritants of everyday life. But in business, the Know-It-All Syndrome can be remarkably self-defeating and counterproductive.

I once sat in on a meeting headed by a fairly effective executive who was a notorious know-it-all. He was smart, charming, and one of the shrewdest negotiators I've ever met. But he had an overwhelming need to display these talents constantly to the world. It cropped up in everything he said.

I'll never forget how he opened the meeting, where several key associates had gathered to discuss the future of a costly project.

He said, "We want to close down the Florida project, don't we?"

The meeting, for all intents and purposes, was over that moment—because it was obvious to everyone that he had already made up his mind. He gave away the answer he was looking for in his question. He was inviting people to agree, not argue. I suspect he left that meeting convinced that he had participated in a free and open exchange of information.

I can't help thinking that this executive would be twice as effective if he learned to suppress his own brilliance on occasion and let others demonstrate theirs. What harm would there have been in asking, "Do we want to shut down the Florida project?"

As stifling as the know-it-all can be within an organization, he is far more dangerous outside, particularly in situations where customers rely on him and set themselves up to be disappointed. Quite often, the problem begins in the way the salesman asks questions.

The head of an industrial supply company I know says that he is always reminding his sales executives—some of whom are very smart and often do know more than the customer—that salesmanship is a two-step process:

Step One: Ask very specific questions.

Step Two: Wait for the answer.

The know-it-alls, he suggests, forget Step Two.

"A good salesman," claims this man, "will ask, 'How many gallons per minute does this system need?'—and listen to the answer.

"The know-it-all salesman says, 'This system needs thirty-five gallons per minute, doesn't it?'—and the uninformed customer thinks he really knows!

"The result is disastrous. The customer comes back, either angry or disappointed, because what we sold him isn't 100 percent right. And there's the know-it-all salesman greeting him and saying, 'But you told me thirty-five gallons per minute . . .' "

ENDING THE ENDLESS CONVERSATION

To busy executives, few business situations are more stressful than being trapped in a conversation that should have ended minutes earlier, but didn't. Even seconds seem like hours if you have other things to do but are too polite to cut the other person off.

Many trapped listeners resort to body language—they squirm, tap fingers, scribble notes, reach for the phone, nod their heads in agreement—but the effect, at best, is unpredictable. Someone too dense to pick up your verbal clues is not apt to read the nonverbal ones.

Here are three lines that should bring a swift conclusion to dialogues that have overstayed their welcome.

1. "YOU'LL HAVE TO GET ME OUT OF THIS CONVERSATION."

This is a euphemism for "Enough!" but few people feel stung by it. If you frame the ending of the discussion as a favor they can do for you, most people will be very happy to oblige.

2. "LET ME SEE IF I CAN HELP YOU GET WHERE YOU SEEM TO BE GOING."

This is an interruption that both implies "I understand" and "I can help you." Use it when people interminably restate the same idea in different ways. If you promise to help them, few will mind the interruption.

127

3. "TELL ME WHAT YOU THINK WE SHOULD DO."

Most people prefer to talk about problems because it's easier than finding solutions. They claim that they need to discuss a problem but actually want to conjecture about every permutation that could have happened if they had done this or that. These people are reliving the past (at your expense) and avoiding the future (also at your expense).

This phrase works as a challenge. It asks for a solution, and either forces the person to rise to the occasion or rise to leave.

WHAT'S RIGHT AND WRONG WITH THE TELEPHONE

Most people agree that the telephone is the greatest business tool at our disposal. If you asked people why, though, they might not agree as easily.

To some people, the telephone's most interesting feature is that it lets them communicate with anyone, anytime. Armed with a telephone directory, they have access to the world. (To some people, of course, this is a mixed blessing, particularly when it means they can be reached anytime by people they would rather avoid.)

To salespeople, the phone is the ultimate timesaver. It dramatically reduces, if not quite eliminates, the time-consuming need to travel to make a sale.

To others, the telephone's most interesting feature is its stark simplicity. All you need to start a business is a desk and a phone. (With the emergence of the cellular phone, you don't even need the desk.)

But to me, the greatest advantage of the telephone is its most obvious feature: *the party on the other end of the line cannot see you.* If you can maintain your concentration and poise on the phone, it doesn't matter what circumstances you find yourself in. You could be lounging in a bubble bath at home or surrounded by mayhem at the office, but the other party on the end of the line neither knows nor cares. The only evidence the other party has is your voice. If you can control that, you're conducting business as usual.

It's amazing how many people forget that.

They'll let an upsetting situation earlier in the day spill over into their telephone calls. They'll sound sullen, distracted, or irritable. That's understandable, of course. Few people can compartmentalize their emotions perfectly from one situation to another. The problem, however, is that the other party can quickly sense their foul mood or distraction and, with no other evidence to go on, concludes that it is intentionally directed at him or her.

I see this most often in secretaries. Admittedly, a secretary's patience with telephone calls is more sorely tested day in and day out than that of any executive. After all, part of a secretary's job is to field all the calls that no one else wants. If a secretary is under intense pressure to finish typing a twenty-five-page report, the completion of which is interrupted repeatedly by irrelevant or low-priority incoming calls, it's understandable that some of that stress might creep into the secretary's phone manner. If you've ever had to deal with a rude or obstructive secretary—whose only excuse for such testy conduct is "I've had a very rough day!"—you know the drill.

The best secretaries are courteous and efficient on the phone all the time, regardless of the pressure or chaos around them. By force of habit, they can assume a calm, professional, curt, or testy demeanor every time the phone rings.

What puzzles me is why so many otherwise smart executives don't have the same phone savvy as their secretaries. I've had phone conversations with countless executives where I could immediately tell whether they were angry, distracted, exhausted, frustrated, or unprepared to deal with me at that moment. If it isn't obvious from the tone of their voice, they will come out and tell me. They'll tell me that they're tired from a long day of meetings. They'll tell me that they're mad at their boss. They'll even describe the disarray on their desk when they can't find their notes.

Yet those qualities are precisely the sort of things that no one should reveal on the phone (unless there is a tactical reason to do so). Not only does it erase the phone's they-can't-see-you advantage, but if I know how someone feels and they don't have a clue what's going through my mind, I feel I have the edge in that conversation.

The biggest mistake people make on the phone is not letting their voice do the work. As I've said, the voice can reveal a variety of emotional states. But many people never think about the image they want to project or how effectively they're coming across.

Before I reach for the phone, I automatically pause for a split second to collect my thoughts and decide what I want to convey solely through my voice. It's a habit to me now, and it's a good habit.

For example, if I'm talking to someone I haven't seen in a few weeks, I always remind myself to be enthusiastic. For some strange reason, people tend to be more compliant and pleasant when they hear that I'm really glad to be talking to them.

If I'm in a hurry, I'll start off by announcing that I only have a few minutes to talk. I find that tends to focus the other party; they get to the point quickly. It also makes me appear less rude when I have to abruptly end the call, since I've already alerted the other side. It's certainly preferable to hanging on the phone, saying nothing but "yes" (the verbal equivalent of drumming your fingers in a meeting), and wishing the other party would stop talking so I could move on to other things.

These examples—show enthusiasm in your voice and tell them your time is limited—may seem patently obvious, like remembering to be polite on the phone. And yet millions of people ignore them, just as millions of people forget to be polite every day. If you want to be more effective on the phone, take a look at your phone habits. Are you taking advantage of the fact that the other party can't see you? Or are you giving that advantage away from the things you say and the way you say them?

The Trouble with Selling on the Phone

Not long ago, one of our executives surprised me with his appraisal of a promising saleswoman. The way he described it, she was effective in every area except closing the deal. Although

131

she is terrific at cold calling and breaking through to people on the phone, she had not yet discovered the knack for impressing people in person.

This surprised me because, for most salespeople, the opposite is true: They're great in person, and not-so-great on the phone.

It certainly applies to me. I am much more comfortable selling to someone one-on-one and "in the flesh" than I am doing so over the telephone.

There are good reasons for this. The telephone, by its very nature, presents so many obstacles to effective salesmanship, it's a wonder any deals get done at all.

OBSTACLE #1: YOU CAN'T SEE THE OTHER PERSON.

I realize that two pages before, I argued that the fact that the other person can't see you is one of the phone's biggest advantages.

But this feature is also the phone's biggest obstacle. In effect, it means you're selling blind. You can't look into the other person's eyes or study the changes in his facial expression as you make your proposal. You can't survey his office, ask about that tennis trophy in the corner, admire his fine Zegna suit, or discuss where his two daughters (pictured on his desk) should go to summer camp. All these nuances enhance the connection between you and the customer—and you can't pick them up on the phone.

OBSTACLE #2: PEOPLE PREFER TO MAKE RATHER THAN TAKE CALLS.

If you call someone, you're doing so at your convenience, not theirs. As a result, nine times out of ten, you're getting them at a bad time (if you get them at all). Either they're doing something else or they're not prepared to talk to you. Whatever the reason—and I'm assuming that your call actually goes through and that you haven't landed in "voice jail"—the circumstances for your conversation are hardly ideal for persuading them to buy something from you.

OBSTACLE #3: THERE IS NO FLEXIBILITY ON TIME.

If you play a round of golf with a customer, you know you have five hours to say what you have to say. At lunch or dinner, you have two hours. Over drinks you have sixty minutes. In a face-to-face meeting, you have at least thirty minutes. You don't get that luxury on the telephone. On phone conversations, the clock is always ticking, always rushing you to hurry up and make your pitch. Even when you have actually determined how much time the person on the other end of the line has to talk to you, there's always the legitimate fear that the conversation will end at any moment, and that the other party will cut you off to take another more important call. (How many times has this happened to you?) These, too, are not ideal circumstances for selling. Which leads to . . .

OBSTACLE #4. YOU HAVE TO BE FRONTAL ON THE PHONE.

And being frontal is not always the best way to persuade people. But the phone usually doesn't leave you any other option.

If you're calling someone for the first time, you basically have sixty to ninety seconds to make your case. In that time, you have to establish your bona fides ("Hi, I'm Mark McCormack calling from IMG."), explain why you're calling ("We represent Client X."), provide references if necessary ("Joe Smith suggested I call you."), and hint at a benefit to the party you're calling ("We have an idea that might interest you.").

Under these conditions, is it any wonder why so many salespeople sound like fast-talking, finger-snapping con artists trying to sell you tidal wave insurance?

Despite these objections, the telephone is still inarguably the greatest business tool at your disposal. It gives you universal access to anyone else with a phone number (and, for better or worse, makes you universally accessible to them, too). It's also a terrific timesaver. After all, not every conversation needs to be conducted in person.

What you have to appreciate, though, is that the phone is not necessarily the greatest *sales* tool.

In my mind, the telephone's greatest strength as a selling tool is to establish your next face-to-face meeting with the prospect. You shouldn't expect to achieve anything more than that.

At least, that's how I use it in cold-calling situations. In my experience, you'll never close a complex deal over the phone. For that matter, you might not even pique the prospect's interest. An in-person meeting is the best you should hope for with that first call.

If you expect any more from this simple device, you're not only overestimating the selling power of the telephone, you're also underestimating the power of showing up in person.

MASTERING THE ART OF THE FIVE-MINUTE CONVERSATION

I was marveling not long ago about a literary agent who works for one of our competitors. It seemed no matter where I turned, I was always reading about her pulling off an impressive book or movie deal for one of her clients. I was amazed not only by the size of the deals but by their frequency. How, I wondered, was she able to deal with so many clients and keep them happy.

I know that representing authors can be very labor-intensive. You need to spend hours reading what they write and devote even more hours talking to them in person or on the phone. They need constant pampering. They expect you to make intelligent suggestions about their writing, which assumes that you have set aside several hours to read their most recent manuscript. They also expect you to be on top of every detail in their business affairs.

If you have to do this for a dozen writers, you have your hands full. But this woman was operating in this manner for several dozen authors.

I was not only amazed by her efficiency but curious about how she did it. So I asked one of her former colleagues, "What's her secret?"

135

"It's simple really," he said. "She is a master of the five-minute conversation. When you talk with her, you always get the feeling that you've said everything that needed to be said, that you've eaten a whole meal, not just nibbled on appetizers. You know that she's hurrying you along, but you don't mind because you don't hang up hungry."

This ex-colleague didn't have any brilliant insights about *how* she accomplished this feat. But I suspect she was doing some or all of the following.

1. WATCH THE CLOCK.

Before you can have shorter conversations, you have to make a conscious decision to control the length of your conversations. And before you can make that decision, you have to accept that shorter conversations are good for you and your business.

If you're in any sort of sales position these days, you're probably spending the bulk of your time communicating with people over the phone. Talking to people is how you make sales. If you want to sell more, you need to talk to more people. You can do this in one of two ways.

First, you can work longer hours. Of course, at some point you run out of time; there are only twenty-four hours in a day and not all those hours are good for reaching people.

Or, you can become more efficient with the conversations you're already having. If you spend an hour chewing the fat with someone, you're losing precious time—time that could have been spent having a dozen five-minute conversations with a dozen different people.

It's not a complicated equation. The shorter the conversation, the more people you reach. And in sales, the more people you reach, the more people you can convert into buyers.

Amazingly, a lot of salespeople have a tough time accepting this. They think that every conversation needs to be an open-ended bonding experience. They're afraid to cut the dialogue short because it might offend the other party. That's not necessarily true, which leads to the next point.

2. GO EASY ON THE BONDING RITUALS.

Once you start clocking your conversations, you must weigh the balance between productive conversation (i.e., dialogue that covers the business points) and personal conversation (i.e., dialogue that establishes and enhances your relationship).

Obviously, it would be a cold, charmless world if all of us restricted our conversations to business points, if we stated our position, listened to the other party's response, and then hung up. Every conversation can use a few warm "bonding gestures," even if they are as trite or ritualistic as "How are the kids?" or "How was your vacation?"

The problem for most people is that they spend too much time on these bonding rituals and, worse, they don't do it intelligently. The biggest error: asking questions that invite interminable answers. With a little thought, you can shave down your personal comments to one or two brief statements and still create a "bonding experience."

I noticed this a few weeks ago when I dined at a wonderful restaurant called Longhi's in Maui. I had not seen the owner, Bob Longhi, in five years, but he wandered over to our table, called my wife Betsy by name, recognized me before I had to introduce myself, and made reference to the fact that the weather in Hawaii was certainly better than the chilly climate in Cleveland (where our company is headquartered). He said all the right things to demonstrate that he knows what's going on and to make us feel welcome and special. And he did it all in forty seconds.

That's not a bad standard to shoot for. A big part of mastering the five-minute conversation is mastering this sort of instant bonding ritual.

3. FRAME THE TIME.

It's not enough to watch the clock on your conversations. You also have to let the other party know that the clock is ticking.

This is the biggest reason people get trapped in long, open-ended conversations. They don't frame the length of the discussion for the other party with an opening statement about how much time they have to talk. But they should.

You have a far better chance of having a five-minute conversation if you announce, "I only have five minutes to talk," than if you don't.

4. MAKE CALLS, DON'T TAKE CALLS.

It's a lot easier to establish *your* agenda if you're placing the call rather than taking it.

But if you make the call, be sure to have something substantive—and preferably positive—to pass on to the other party.

In my early years I used to have incredibly long phone conversations with some of my clients. And they weren't always pleasant or productive. They'd call me up with a laundry list of questions and complaints, many of which I wasn't prepared to answer or address at the time of the call. It took me a while to realize that these phone calls would be considerably more productive if I placed them at my convenience.

It took me even longer to appreciate that clients called me because they were eager to hear some good news. But eventually I noticed that if I opened the discussion with a positive bulletin, the clients were less likely to pepper me with questions about irrelevant matters.

A part of it, I'm sure, was that they wanted to know that I was working hard for them. Calling them rather than waiting for them to call me addressed that concern.

Calling with good news kept the conversations short. I guess that's human nature. If you open with good news, people are less likely to prolong the conversation to hear what else you have to say, particularly if it might *not* be so positive.

5. SCHEDULE THE NEXT CONVERSATION.

If you have to cut someone off abruptly, they will accept it more graciously if you say, "Why don't we discuss this again next Tuesday at ten o'clock."

People will gladly end a conversation when you want them to if they know they will have a chance to talk to you again in the near future. So tell them.

CHAPTER 7

Getting It Down
in Writing

MAKING YOUR POINT WITHOUT
MAKING A MESS

In our organization, I get "copied" on virtually every document. Consequently, I have a profound appreciation for short memos. My favorite memo is one sentence long. My second favorite is two sentences, and so on. My executives know this. If they want to win me over, they better do it quickly. Lengthy memos don't impress me; they worry me.

The following pointers won't transform you into a prose stylist, but they can improve the clarity and effectiveness of your memos.

141

1. DO YOU HAVE A POINT?

Someone told me that the toughest memos to write deliver one of these messages:

- This is how you do it.

- I want to sell you.

- I goofed.

- I have some bad news for you.

- I did a great job.

- Dear Boss, you're wrong.

- This is my demand.

- This is how you rate.

I would read a memo that began with any one of these sentences.

2. DOES IT READ BETTER FROM THE END?

David Mamet, the playwright and screenwriter, says that all good movie scripts must divide neatly into three coherent acts. In attempting to explain this three-act theory to a screenwriting class, Mamet recalled a news headline in the *New York Post* which read, "Boy Cuts Off Father's Head, Cuts Off Parakeet's Head, Then Cuts Off Lizard's Head." The secret to good screenwriting, says Mamet, is knowing to cut the father's head off last.

A lot of memos would be more persuasive if their first and last paragraphs were switched.

This is certainly true of writers who use their memos to duplicate their thought processes. Their memos are written like blow-by-blow chronologies of how they thought a problem through. They read like algebraic proofs, complete with a neat and tidy conclusion at memo's end.

They'd read much better (and actually get read) if that concluding paragraph came at the beginning rather than the end. In other words, if you have a new way to cut costs, announce it in sentence one. If you're asking for a new computer, say so at the start. Don't drop your bombshell at memo's end; it may blow up in your face.

3. IS IT SHORT ENOUGH?

Short words, short sentences, short paragraphs work. Trust me.

Weigh every word against your readers' time and attention span. Too many writers write for themselves, using their memos to duplicate their thought processes. People don't need a blow-by-blow chronology of how you thought a problem through—and they certainly don't want to read about it. They want the nugget that inspired the memo, and they want it fast. If you have a way to cut costs, announce it in sentence one. If you're asking for a new computer, say so at the start.

4. DO YOU HAVE ENOUGH QUALIFIERS?

In their classic primer, *The Elements of Style*, William Strunk and E.B. White make the point that if you want your writing to be strong and convincing, you should "avoid the use of qualifiers."

Words like *rather*, *very*, *little*, and *pretty*, they advised, "are the leeches that infest the pond of prose, sucking the blood of words. The constant use of the adjective little (except to indicate size) is particularly debilitating; we should all try to do a little better, we should all be very watchful of this rule, for it is a rather important one, and we are pretty sure to violate it now and then."

Much as I esteem Strunk and White, I think the opposite is true when you are writing memos to your peers or subordinates.

If you want to achieve a positive result, you should go out of your way to insert qualifiers and appeasing statements in a memo. It may weaken your writing style, but it will strengthen your position.

If you are irritated with someone, don't confront them by writing, "How could you let this happen?" That will only make them defensive. You're much better off saying, "I realize you're very busy, and that you probably didn't attend to this matter personally. But a problem has come up and I really need your help with it."

If you were the reader, which of these approaches would appeal to you?

5. TRY TO EXPRESS, NOT IMPRESS.

In most memos, writes William K. Zinsser in his invaluable book, *On Writing Well*, "the main villain is pomposity. Executives at every level are prisoners of the notion that a simple style reflects a simple mind. Actually, a simple style is the result of hard work and hard thinking; a muddy style reflects a muddy thinker or a person too lazy to organize his thoughts."

6. ARE YOU ON THE OFFENSE OR DEFENSE?

Business memos usually have two purposes—either to project your ideas onto the company or to protect you from other people's ideas. Make your choice before you write a word. Whether you're advancing your cause or defending your turf, your readers won't be clear about it unless you are.

7. BE YOURSELF.

With the best memos, I don't need to see the signature to know who sent it. The writer's identity is there on paper. Unfortunately, for most memo writers it's easier to abandon personality. Instead of trusting their unique way of expressing ideas, they mimic the safe, familiar language of memospeak ("It has been determined that to facilitate increased productivity goals . . .")

Adding personality to a memo is not easy. But you can start by heaping on the personal pronouns such as "I" and "you" and "we" and "our." These are short but very specific words.

The only personal touch to avoid is humor. I say this even though I believe humor is one of the most valuable tools in business. But jokes are best delivered face-to-face. On paper, humor is dangerous because you can't predict how readers will take it.

8. REMOVE THE STINGERS IN WRITING.

One of the more exasperating parts of my job is the fact that I see a lot of the memos and internal correspondence that travel between our far-flung offices. It's exasperating because many of the memos are so counterproductive. Messages intended to inspire cooperation or correct a problem only end up creating more dissension and problems. The biggest culprit is the ill-chosen turn of phrase.

Over the years I've come to the conclusion that not enough people appreciate the tremendous power of the written word.

They blithely toss phrases into their correspondence that are harmless in conversation but have an altogether more chilling effect in writing.

For example, if you tell a colleague face-to-face, "You really messed up," chances are the colleague won't be offended. If he is a friend of yours, he will probably laugh it off and agree with you. But put that sentence in writing and you will be asking for trouble. Your colleague doesn't see the smile on your face or hear the friendly inflection in your voice as you state your opinion. All he sees are the four cold words accusing him of incompetence. Don't be surprised if you get an angry response—in person or in writing.

146

9. GET A SECOND OPINION.

Most people are so engrossed in the message they are trying to convey that they forget to step out of themselves and think about the reader. The most effective communicators try to visualize the person reading and reacting to their writing. If they're not sure how some of their stronger comments will be received, they get a second opinion before they send it off, usually from a friend or associate.

I remember when one of our New York executives asked his secretary to look over a quick fax he was sending to an executive in our Hong Kong office who needed instructions on how to handle a delicate contract renewal. It was a simple one-paragraph message, but he wanted to make sure it didn't sound peremptory, as if he was dumping a tricky assignment on the Hong Kong office.

"What's the big deal?" asked the secretary. "How could anybody be offended by this?"

The executive pointed out to her that you have to be very careful with memos to foreign lands or to people you don't see or talk to on a regular basis. Even the simplest messages can be misinterpreted.

"It's like humor in print," he explained. "A joke in person can be funny. A joke on paper can be insulting."

The secretary thought her boss was being overcautious.

Coincidentally, the next day, this same secretary received a memo from another secretary in our London office. It, too, was a simple one-paragraph message, saying in effect: "I understand you are the person now handling the transfer of reports on the XYZ project. Please be sure to attend to this at the beginning of each month. Please let me know if there are any problems fulfilling these responsibilities."

There is nothing overtly offensive or bossy in this memo. Yet the secretary, I'm told, was offended. She even showed it to her boss, saying, "Who does this woman think she is?"

All the executive could do was gently point out that next time maybe she would read *his* memos with a little more understanding.

10. REMOVE THE EMOTION.

Whenever President Harry Truman wrote an angry letter, he would put it away in his desk for twenty-four hours to see if he felt the same way the next day.

This may be the most important rule of all. Memos and letters sent in the heat of emotion probably create more misunderstandings than any other form of correspondence. Unless you are intentionally trying to anger someone or make a point in some political infighting, never send an angry memo until you've had a chance to sleep on it. If you feel the same way twenty-four hours later, at least you will know the memo's sting was not unintentional.

11. USE BULLETS, FOR THE FOLLOWING REASONS:

- To organize your thoughts

- To simplify complex subjects

- To highlight the main point

- To break up the page visually

- To give readers a breather

12. Use a thesaurus.

The quickest way to improve your writing is to use more colorful verbs. You'll find hundreds of vivid verbs in a thesaurus (the use of which is nothing to be ashamed of). Sprinkle fresh verbs into your memos and your language will have precision and action. Whenever possible, use active verbs ("I recommend") rather than passive verbs ("It is recommended"). Eliminate the passive voice and you'll silence the biggest source of bombast in memos.

13. Neatness counts.

And it counts a lot. Only sloppy executives send out sloppy memos. Perfect grammar and perfect proofreading display professionalism and courtesy to the reader. Even if your suggestions are shot down, you will earn credibility.

Avoiding the Errors That Make You Look Foolish

I began this book by being slightly dismissive of perfect grammar. I contend that using "whom" rather than "who" correctly won't necessarily help you achieve most business goals.

But I'd be remiss if I didn't point out the flip side to my seemingly glib dismissal of perfect grammar and elegant language. The flip side is this: Although perfect grammar and a dazzling vocabulary won't necessarily make you more effective in business, their absence does have an effect. Grossly imperfect grammar and clumsy use of the language can make you look stupid.

And that's not good.

Although I realize I can't make readers smarter about grammar and writing overnight, I can help them avoid looking stupid. It's a simple matter of error avoidance. For example:

1. KNOW YOUR BLIND SPOTS.

I know I have certain blind spots when it comes to the English language. I'm not only careless with the proper use of "who" and "whom" or "that" and "which," but I also split my infinitives ("to *personally* look into the matter" should be "to look into *personally*") and use plural verbs with singular nouns ("None of us *are* . . ." should really be "None of us *is* . . . "). These are not my only grammatical sins; they're the ones I'm willing to admit to (note the sinful deployment of the preposition at the end of this last sentence).

The good news is that I know this about myself. That's why, before this document you are currently reading ever reaches your hands, I have it reviewed for grammatical correctness by a former Latin instructor in our Cleveland office. I may have blind spots about English, but she doesn't.

I can't guarantee that my thoughts here will always make me sound clever or wise, but with her reviewing my sentences, I know I won't sound stupid.

I recommend this to everyone. Before you rush out that important piece of writing, show it to someone you trust or admire. If that individual points out one typographical error, one misspelling, one abuse of the English language, or one lapse in logic, the exercise is well worth it.

2. NEVER USE A WORD YOU DON'T KNOW.

I recently met with a CEO who was eager to get more exposure for his company's name through sports sponsorships. He was also eager to get more exposure for himself and grew quite animated when he learned we had a speaker's bureau that could secure him paid speaking appearances.

He claimed he had a powerful message for would-be entrepreneurs and that his speeches were laced with humor. Audiences appeared to respond to, as he put it, his "self-depreciating approach."

I'm sure he meant "self-deprecating." He said it without a smile or any hint that he was making an extremely subtle pun. And in that moment when he mispronounced the word, my opinion of him diminished slightly. A speaker who wants to command hefty fees does not go around mangling the English language.

If you're not sure what a word means or how to pronounce it, don't use it. You'll only look foolish to the people you're trying to impress.

151

3. Delete unnecessary words you don't need.

Welcome to the Department of Redundancy Department. This is the place where people receive *free gifts*, where they learn to *plan ahead*, where they compete with *foreign imports*, attend *group meetings*, and share *personal opinions* that range from the *honest truth* about a *new breakthrough* to the *current status* of the *different varieties* . . .

I hope you get the point. The error here is wordiness. In each of the italicized phrases above, one of the words is tagging along for the ride and should be jettisoned. All gifts are free—that's what makes them gifts. You can't plan backward. Imports are inherently foreign. Meetings, by definition, are a group activity (they can't be done solo). I don't know any opinions that aren't personal. There's no such thing as the dishonest truth. All breakthroughs are new. Status implies that it's current. Varieties are never the same.

4. Use a semicolon with extreme caution.

Punctuation involves a lot of rules, some of them simple, some ornery. Fortunately, there's enough leeway in the rules that omitting or misplacing a comma doesn't necessarily brand you as an illiterate.

In my mind, the one piece of punctuation that can make you look foolish is the semicolon. It's the most abused form of punctuation, invariably because people ask the semicolon to do jobs that rightfully belong to commas, colons, and periods.

As a rule, you should use a semicolon to separate independent thoughts that are closely related to each other and that are not separated by a conjunction (e.g., "These are not my only grammatical sins; they're the ones I'm willing to admit to.").

You can also use it to separate phrases or items in a list in which the phrases or items contain confusing commas (e.g., I visited three cities last week: Cheyenne, Wyoming; Terre Haute, Indiana; Port Chester, New York.).

That's about it for the semicolon. Anything else is abuse—and makes you look foolish.

So don't sprinkle semicolons into your documents because you think they look good. The proper use of a semicolon is a sign that you really know your way around a document. Until you know how to use it, don't.

5. NEVER MISSPELL THE READER'S NAME.

Hey, no one's perfect. Misspellings (and typos) creep into any document, even with the advent of spell-checking programs in every word processor.

But there's no excuse for misspelling your intended reader's name. Spelling a name correctly doesn't make an impression; it's expected. Spelling it wrong does—and it's not positive.

6. DARE TO BE PRECISE.

The most maddening error has nothing to do with redundancies, punctuation, spelling, or pronunciation. It has to do with precision.

It's not enough to be understood. You must also communicate in a way that you cannot possibly be misunderstood. To achieve that, you need to remove all the vague, imprecise lo-cutions from your writing.

Don't fall into the trap of saying, "I'll get back to you in a *few days.*" Be specific. Say *three days* or *3 P.M., June 3.*

Don't refer to a *recent letter* when you can call it *the let-ter of April 19.*

Don't promise *quick turnaround* when you can deliver *twenty-four-hour turnaround."*

Don't demand something *as soon as possible* if you need it *by the 13th.*

If you dare to be precise, you will not only reduce the chances of being misunderstood, you will also look more but-toned-up and on top of the situation. In other words, you will look smarter.

THE ART OF THE SELF-SERVING MEMO

The headline above is slightly misleading. The terrible truth about memos is that all of them are self-serving. Whether you use a memo to persuade another person, stake out your turf, im-part information, or acknowledge someone else's contribu-tion, the raw impulse behind it is the same: Advancement or protection. You either want to move forward or protect your-self. If memos didn't serve this function, why would people spend so much time writing them?

Some memos, of course, are more self-serving than oth-ers. The paradox is that the more transparently self-serving the memo, the less effective it is. When people see ego and naked ambition on display in a memo, they tend to resist it. Think about the last time someone baldly attacked you or someone you know in a memo. That's how memo wars begin.

Conversely, the most effective memos go to great lengths to obscure their self-serving purpose. In their most perfect form, such memos leave the reader with no idea that he or she is being attacked, persuaded, or manipulated. You can't call yourself an effective communicator if you don't appreciate this and if you don't know how to write such memos. Here are two of my favorites.

1. THE "STATE OF THE RELATIONSHIP" MEMO

Here's a quiz. Name the six most important business relationships you have. When was the last time you wrote a thoroughly detailed memo to each one reviewing the state of your relationship?

If you're like most people, I suspect the answer is never. I can see why. You probably see or talk to these half-dozen key people on a daily or weekly basis throughout the year. You're up to speed on each other's activities. Why do you need a memo that restates what you already know?

I don't see it that way. In fact, the constant contact with your key relationships is an argument for writing a "state of the relationship" memo. Just as it's hard to notice that a friend you see everyday has lost weight or gradually changed her hair color, it's also difficult to detect changes in a business relationship that revolves around daily or weekly contact. If you're regularly talking to the same people, you tend to focus on the here-and-now; problems (and the solutions you provided) from the near or distant past fall by the wayside. Both sides need a "state of the relationship" memo—if only to appreciate how far the two of you have traveled together.

In the course of writing my next business primer, *On Communicating*, I reviewed several years of memos I had written. Without question, the memos I am most proud of (and which required the most time and effort) are the eight to ten "state of the relationship" memos I write each year.

For example, I wrote a twenty-six-page single-spaced memo reviewing all the activities we did for a client during a two-year period for which we did not commission a fee. Although I didn't include an invoice with my memo (or even discuss money), the net result was an additional six-figure fee for our company.

Another memo devoted nine of its fifteen pages to reviewing a television contract negotiation for a valued sports federation. My goal was to demonstrate how hard we worked and what obstacles we had to overcome to secure a decent contract in a soft television market. I didn't come out and say, "Hey, we did a great job!" I didn't have to. Nine pages describing our strategy gets the same point across.

In each case, the memos were written chiefly to summarize a relationship—to clear the air, review facts, outline our position, and give the other side a chance to say, "No, that's not the way we see it." If the memo leads to a stronger relationship or a financial payoff, that's a pleasant bonus. It's also the essence of a well-executed self-serving memo.

If you're not writing a half-dozen or more of these "state of the relationship" memos each year—to your most important accounts, your mentors, your best professional "friends," perhaps to your boss—isn't it time you did?

2. The third party memo

Survivors of corporate warfare know that you should never say something negative about a third party in a memo that you wouldn't want that third party to see—because as night follows day, the third party will eventually see or hear of that memo.

I like to turn this strange but immutable fact of corporate life on its head. If it's true that a third party always sees the offending document that you wrote to someone else, why not write your memos acknowledging that a third party will see it? You will make your point without offending anyone.

As the CEO of a company, I'm a great believer in taking memos addressed to me and passing them on to interested third parties. I realized this years ago when a crisis came up involving a close friend with whom our company did business. One of our accountants concluded that we were being dramatically overcharged by my friend's company when all along we thought we were getting a preferred rate. I didn't feel comfortable accusing my friend of gouging us. For all I know, he wasn't aware of the problem. So I let our accountant do the dirty work. I simply took the accountant's internal memo outlining the overcharges, attached a note saying, "What's going on?" and sent it to my friend. Our two companies settled the problem amicably, without damaging our friendship.

Since then I've become an afficionado of memos written for third parties. I pass them along all the time. I often ask people to rewrite internal memos specifically because I intend to show them to someone else. I'm also adept at spotting those occasions when I'm the third party and people are intentionally writing memos to someone else but for me to see.

What's interesting is that I'm not offended by this self-serving tactic, even when I'm aware of it. Memos written for a third party's eyes are a terrific way to make a controversial or provocative point without being confrontational. They probably create more peaceful solutions than any other document in the workplace.

Dr. Jekyll in Person, Mr. Hyde on Paper

One of our senior executives once accused me of having a split personality when it came to communicating with our employees. He claimed I was Dr. Jekyll when I dealt with people in person or by phone. That is, I kept in touch with key employees frequently and regularly, and in all these verbal encounters I was polite, solicitous, interested, and responsive.

However, he contended, something strange happened to me when I communicated with these same employees by memo. I turned into Mr. Hyde. I became imperious, condescending, and caustic. What irked this executive was a specific memo I had written in which I chided a group of executives with the phrase, ". . . with reference to how the 'real world' is working . . ." as if I regarded them as either incompetent or completely insensitive to everyday business conditions.

This executive suggested that I might not be aware that I assumed this haughty tone in my memos. He also suggested that I should try to be more consistent, and that there was a great virtue in being as polite in writing as I was in person.

I agree that it may have been intemperate to suggest our people were not in touch with the "real world." I could have chosen words with less sting.

But I don't agree that I'm not aware of the power of the written word. I knew exactly what I was doing when I wrote those words.

I also don't agree about the virtue of being consistent. In fact, if anything, I was going overboard to be inconsistent. I wanted these people to appreciate my displeasure, and the jarring contrast of the memo with my everyday polite personal contacts with them would certainly convey that message.

I have always thought that it's much better to be unpredictable in communicating with people. It keeps people on their toes and punctures even the slightest form of complacency. If you're predictable, in person or on paper, eventually your words will lose all their meaning.

However, I do agree with the executive's larger point. There is an immense difference between criticizing people in writing and in person. After all, you can't deliver a caustic memo with a smile on your face.

It's one thing for you to say to a subordinate, "Don't you think it's the height of stupidity that no one at our company has visited the XYZ Corporation's offices since they renewed their contract with us?" If you are smiling when you say this, the subordinate can see that you're making a point but you're not too upset about it. Yet if you make that same comment in a memo, and especially if you send copies to his colleagues, that "height of stupidity" phrase will stand out like a slap in the face.

If that's the effect you're trying to achieve, fine. It will have an even greater impact because it is so unexpected, because you have been unpredictable.

Unfortunately, many people are careless with the written word. They don't use their letters and memos to achieve a desired effect. Instead, they write to vent their emotions and frustrations. All their hostilities seem to come out when they get a pen in their hand. The biggest culprit is the gratuitous phrase—the odd expression or sentence that makes the writer feel better but has an altogether different effect on the reader.

I once asked one of our senior executives to draft a memo for my signature in which we were going to give an employee a bonus but also were going to withhold some monies he owed the company. The memo this executive wrote outlined the bonus and described the deduction of monies due us as something "which you know has been a source of irritation to me for some time."

I suppose adding that little dig at the end made the executive feel good. But I didn't send the memo that way.

I simply announced the bonus and explained the deduction. After all, who cares if it has been a source of irritation to me? The reader gets the point. He can't argue about the fact that he's getting a surprise bonus, which is good news. Nor can he be mad about the deduction, which he knows he owes us. But mentioning my irritation is gratuitous—and particularly inappropriate in a memo where my intention is to congratulate the employee for a job well done.

There's nothing wrong with being a split personality in your communications. Depending on the circumstances, either Jekyll or Hyde may be called for. Just make sure that you know which role you are playing—and why.

Making Sure Your Proposals Get Read

I still write many of our company's sales proposals. I should probably delegate more of this but, frankly, a proposal over my signature has a greater chance of being read at a company that doesn't know us well. Here is a short course on writing proposals.

1. Keep it short.

What applies to memos applies to proposals, too. Before you mail your twenty-four-page masterpiece, ask yourself: When was the last time you got as far as page 24 of someone else's proposal?

2. Give them your best ideas, not all your ideas.

I often think a proposal is judged by the worst idea in it; at least that's the one someone at the prospect's company always seems to pick on. You never get a second chance to send a first proposal. Save your off-the-wall suggestions for later when they know you better.

3. Remember your reader.

People often overlook the importance of a person's rank or position in determining how they should communicate with them.

Different people need to be communicated with in different ways about the same subjects. Your boss expects to be informed. Your peers want to be included. Your subordinates need to be instructed.

For example, senior executives in our company know by now that, in communicating with me, I only need a few sentences on most subjects. I don't need an elaborate chapter-and-verse historical summary of "How I did that deal." I want simple information on the order of (a) what was sold, (b) by whom, (c) to whom, and (d) for how much.

That sort of brevity isn't appropriate or constructive with peers and subordinates.

Your peers deserve more details, not only to feel included but also because they might learn something and can offer suggestions that could improve future transactions.

Subordinates, on the other hand, often have huge gaps in their understanding of your business. This is the sort of information that you gradually take for granted as you ascend in the company. It's important that you take time out to give them the complete picture of a situation or relationship that started long ago.

This communication hierarchy of bosses, peers, and subordinates applies in corporate sales as well. When you approach other companies, tailor your sales presentation with the following in mind:

- Bosses (CEOs, senior officers) want strategic answers: Why should we be in this market? What's the long-term impact? What trends are we anticipating?

- Peers (vice presidents, department heads) want tactical answers. How much will this cost? How will it make my job easier? How will it improve my bottom line?

- Subordinates (line managers, engineers) want technical details. How does it work? Will it last? Does it fit?

As a rule, there's no percentage in talking long-term strategy with technicians, and there's no excuse for boring the CEO with nuts-and-bolts details.

4. CANVASS YOUR COLLEAGUES.

When it comes to proposals, I think it's foolish to work alone. So I brainstorm before I write. I'm always asking each of our executives for a dozen ideas that would be appropriate for a new prospect. I then cherry-pick the best suggestions and drop them into my proposal.

5. CREATE A "PROPOSAL RELATIONSHIP."

My favorite proposals are the ones I don't have to write. Instead, an associate writes me a memo on what XYZ Corp. should be doing and I send it on to the company with a cover letter saying, in effect, "Here are some of our internal thoughts which you might find interesting." It gives our proposal the aura of "inside information"—and it always gets read.

CHAPTER 8

Making a Great Speech

Is there anyone out there who doesn't agree that the ability to speak well in public can be a tremendous boon to your career? I'm not suggesting that only great orators can make it to the top in business. On the contrary, some of the most successful CEOs I know happen to be lethally dull public speakers. They are nowhere near as commanding before a large audience as they are in a small group or one-on-one.

However, the converse also applies: I know some people who have risen a lot farther than their brighter and more talented peers simply because of their ability to perform in front of a crowd. So if you don't think that communicating in public is important, think again.

Over the years, I've heard a lot of advice about making a speech. Some is immensely practical, such as the classic speech organizer: "First, tell them what you're going to tell them. Then tell them. Finally, tell them what you've just told them."

A lot, however, is useless: "Relax." "Don't be nervous." "Make the audience like you." "Project a confident personality." These pearls of wisdom certainly sound good. But they are virtually impossible to do. It's like telling a short person to be taller.

The following eleven points cannot only improve your speechmaking, but they have the added virtue of being easy to do.

1. BE NERVOUS.

Fear of public speaking, I'm told, is the number one business phobia.

Yet anyone who isn't a little edgy before a speech is either lying to himself or about to fall on his face. Nerves make you alert, but they also force you to prepare. I've seen some of the most timid, colorless people dazzle an audience because they knew their subject.

I don't think there is such a thing as fear of public speaking. I think it's really a fear of (a) not knowing your subject and (b) being found out.

2. REHEARSE.

The reason ballet dancers work so hard in rehearsal is so that their twenty minutes on stage gives the appearance of hardly working. The goes for same in public speaking. The apparent effortlessness of a speech is inversely proportional to how much effort the speaker put into it. So it's important not only to plan what you're going to say but to rehearse it. Get up and try it out on family, friends, an empty room, or a mirror. As Mark

Twain was fond of saying, "It takes three weeks to prepare a good informal talk." And he was probably underestimating.

3. YOU CAN NEVER HAVE TOO MANY ANECDOTES.

When in doubt tell a story. Even when your delivery leaves something to be desired, if it has a beginning, middle, and end, people will listen.

Anecdotes can be current news or they can be appropriated from history. Believe me, if you can draw an interesting parallel between the Trojan War and competition in your industry, the audience won't care that the story is three thousand years old.

4. SPEAK RATHER THAN READ.

Reading a fully scripted speech is not really "public speaking." It's more like "reading in public," which most people would consider impolite behavior. You're much better off working from notes that hit the main points and cue you to insert off-the-cuff remarks. It forces you to make eye contact with the audience. It also forces you to think about what you're saying. It makes you appear in command of your subject. And it makes you sound like a normal human being.

5. SHAKE HANDS WITH THE AUDIENCE.

There are many ways to get comfortable with your audience and the audience with you.

Most people start out with a joke. Experienced speakers choose a joke that actually has some relevance to their subsequent remarks. But a lot of people don't. They tell a joke to show their human side and to get some interaction between themselves and the audience. These are legitimate goals. But you don't have to rely on a joke.

I know one professional seminarist who starts off his lectures by tossing candy into the audience. It's a crude, obvious device to break down the wall between speaker and audience, but it works every time. It forces people to jump out of their seats to catch the candy. It gets their heart rate up. It's also a nice gesture. People eat the candy.

I know other speakers who begin their talks by giving the audience a quiz. It not only sets up the big themes of the speech, but it gives the speaker a better idea about how smart the audience is. It's also an effective way to turn a stiff, formal gathering into a relaxed free-for-all.

Robert Strauss, the American diplomat and former Ambassador to Russia, starts his addresses on large geopolitical issues with, "Before I begin this speech, I have something to say." People get the one-liner immediately.

Some occasions call for little more than a variation on hello. I remember delivering a eulogy in a church and opening my remarks with a simple, "Good morning." I was surprised (but also warmed) when the congregation in unison returned my greeting with their own, "Good morning." It made an instant connection. I doubt if a business group in a conference hall would have returned my greeting. But in a church, with its call-and-response tradition, it made perfect sense.

My point is, match your opening to the occasion and to the audience, and do it quickly. Once you get your smile, get to work.

6. KNOW YOUR THEME.

I have two themes when I give a speech.

If I'm talking to a student group or a gathering of sales-people, my theme is "common sense." That's what I stand for in business. That's what all my books are about. That's what all my anecdotes aim to illustrate: that applying common sense—i.e., wisdom that you already know—can help you succeed in any situation. I never waver from this theme when I'm handing out advice.

If I'm talking to a group of sports people, my theme is almost as simple: "What happens in America will eventually happen in the rest of the world." This is the principle on which we built our sports marketing business. It's the formula for our expansion into every country. We've never wavered from it in actual practice. So I never waver from it in a speech about our business practices.

If you don't know your overarching theme and, consequently, don't articulate it, don't expect the audience to read your mind or between your lines.

Know your theme and state it boldly.

7. HAVE A PURPOSE.

I began this book with a quick list of the goals of communication. A speech should also have a goal. It can inspire, ennoble, educate, rally, lead, thank, defy, greet, persuade, or defend a position. It can do a lot of other things. But, again, if you don't have a purpose, your audience won't get it either.

8. FIND YOUR RHYTHM.

Pulse or rhythm in a speech varies from person to person. A Baptist minister preaching to his flock can make a sermon sound like the verse and chorus of a pop song.

I can't do that. But I know my limitations. And I know what I'm comfortable with.

I like lists. (Have you noticed that yet?) Lists shape the pulse of my speeches.

If I'm talking about "How to Get Quality in a Personal Services Business," I have seven points to make, and I take the audience by the hand through each one. If I'm identifying "The Next Big Sport," I run through the five criteria that the sport will have to meet.

This method is hardly original with me. The population of business speakers would be reduced by half if no one was allowed to give speeches entitled, "The Ten Forces Shaping the 21st Century Economy" or "Ten Stupid Things Women Do to Mess Up Their Lives."

Lists are a staple (if not a cliché). But they work.

9. MAKE A PHRASE.

A good speech should have at least one phrase that sticks in the audience mind.

I have a ninety-minute speech on selling and negotiating that, for want of a better title, I call "What They Don't Teach You at Harvard Business School." I download dozens of anecdotes from my past during the course of the talk, all to illustrate my commonsense theme. I doubt if the next day the audience remembers 10 percent of what I said. But one phrase always sticks in people's minds. It's when I talk about doing business with friends. I say, "All things being equal, it's great to do business with a friend. In fact, all things being not quite so equal, you should still do business with a friend."

For some reason, people respond to the phrase, "All things being not quite so equal . . ." It has lots of resonance about the importance of building and maintaining relationships.

Experience has taught me the phrase works. So I'm sticking with it.

If you don't have a similar sure-fire expression, I suggest you get one.

10. DON'T OVERSTAY YOUR WELCOME.

Franklin D. Roosevelt had a six-word formula for speeches: "Be sincere, be brief, be seated." You cannot imagine how much better a sixty-minute speech sounds if it only takes thirty minutes to deliver—or how grateful your audience will be toward you if you are the one who can pull off this achievement.

If you have any doubt about leaving a point in or taking it out, choose the latter.

11. WRITE YOUR OWN INTRODUCTION.

I started writing my own introductions some years ago when I discovered that the people introducing me to the audience were basing their comments on severely outdated articles about me and our company. Thus, I'd spend the first part of my talk correcting the introduction, which was hardly the most stirring beginning to a speech and less than gracious to my host.

Self-generated introductions not only eliminated the misinformation but gave me control over how the audience perceived me. My text was carefully calibrated to make me sound like the greatest thing since sliced bread. It generated applause no matter who was reading it. Believe me, that's a very nice greeting when you step up to the podium.

Writing your own introduction isn't an ego trip. It's good business. When you consider how many regard writing as a chore, you're actually doing your host a big favor. Most hosts will read exactly what you have written, word-for-word. If this tactic doesn't get the audience on your side, you have only yourself to blame.

THE NEXT BEST THING
TO BEING FUNNY

I am convinced the two toughest things to do in life are (1) hit a golf ball in the general direction of the hole and (2) be funny in a speech.

Unfortunately, I don't have any miracle cure for either challenge. When I consider all the hours I've spent trying to get that dimpled white ball into the cup, I know there's nothing I can say or write down that will improve anyone's golf game.

It's pretty much the same with being funny in a speech. Humor, like golf, is unnervingly difficult. Being funny is a natural gift, developed early in life. You either can make people laugh—or you can't. You either see the comical side of a situation—or you don't. If you've never been funny in one-on-one situations, it's a sure bet you won't suddenly discover your comic talent in front of a large audience of strangers.

A big part of the problem, of course, is that, even when our material is humorous, few of us possess the performance skills to make the material work. We don't have the voice, timing, delivery, confidence, or overall theatricality to dazzle. We also tend to miscalculate how our alleged "humor" will be received by the audience. The line between funny and flat is thin indeed.

To illustrate the point, consider the hit film, *Four Weddings and a Funeral*, which features several beautifully written speeches.

The first is a toast delivered by the best man Charles (played by Hugh Grant) at the wedding of Angus and Laura. Here is the text:

Ladies and gentlemen, I'm sorry to drag you away from your delicious desserts. There are just one or two little things I feel I should say as best man.

This is only the second time I've ever been a best man. I hope I did the job all right that time. The couple in question at least are still talking to me.

Unfortunately, they're not actually talking to each other. The divorce came through a couple of months ago. But I'm assured it had absolutely nothing to do with me.

Apparently, Paula knew that Pierre had slept with her younger sister before I'd mentioned it in a speech.

The fact that he'd slept with her mother came as a surprise, but I think was incidental to the nightmare of recrimination and violence that became their two-day marriage.

Anyway, enough of that. My job today is to talk about Angus. And there are no skeletons in his cupboard . . .

Or so I thought.

But I'll come on to that in a minute. But I would just like to say this. (Pause)

I am, as ever, in bewildered awe of everyone who makes this kind of commitment that Angus and Laura have made today. I know I couldn't do it. And I think it's wonderful that they can.

So anyway, back to Angus and those sheep.

So, ladies and gentlemen, if you would raise your glasses: The adorable couple.

It's a funny speech. Although I'm sure its humor is aided by Hugh Grant's stylishly bumbling delivery, the toast is re-

174

markable for its audacity and irreverence. We're at a wedding, after all, and the best man is not only talking about adultery and disastrous marriages but seems to suggest some sort of perversion in the groom's past. Yet the toast sidesteps all these self-constructed land mines with a quality that's all too rare in public discourse and, for that matter, any other communication. That quality is charm. It's the next best thing to being funny.

It contrasts dramatically with the film's second toast delivered by the socially awkward (and charmless) Tom at the wedding of Bernard and Lydia:

> When Bernard told me he was getting engaged to Lydia, I congratulated him because all of his other girlfriends had been such complete dogs. Although, may I say how delighted we are to have so many of them here this evening. I'm particularly delighted to see Camilla, who many of you will probably remember as the first person Bernard asked to marry him. If I remember rightly, she told him to 'Sod off!' And lucky for Lydia that she did.

The speech is so comically inept and the humor so wrong-footed that the filmmakers mercifully cut to the next scene.

Prospective speechmakers could do a lot worse than to study the first toast. It's only 238 words long, but it contains virtually all the elements you need to charm an audience (humor may be tough, but all of us can be charming). Those elements are:

1. APOLOGIZE FOR THE INTRUSION.

The toast begins with an apology ("I'm sorry to drag you away from your delicious desserts."). A speech, by definition, is an intrusion on people. Unless the audience has come specifically to hear you talk, they'd rather be doing something else. So it's smart to acknowledge that with an apology—however insincere it may be. It's a maneuver that will immediately win your audience's attention, appreciation, and possibly affection.

2. LOWER THEIR EXPECTATIONS WITH HUMILITY.

It then segues immediately to an admission that the speaker is inexperienced at giving toasts ("This is only the second time I've ever been a best man . . ."). Again, a maneuver designed to charm.

At the start of any speech, a speaker must present his credentials. He must explain what achievements in his past give him the right to intrude on people's ears and the authority to force them to pay attention. In recommending himself to an audience, a speaker should employ as much humility and self-deprecation as possible. The more fun you can poke at yourself, the more people will like you. It makes you seem more like them (even if you aren't).

More important, such humility lowers expectations. If you pump yourself up at the start of a speech, you're only conditioning the audience to expect a speech that matches your high opinion of yourself. That's sometimes hard to live up to. On the other hand, if you poke fun at yourself, the audience doesn't expect as much—and is therefore pleasantly surprised when you deliver the goods.

If you lower the bar, it's easier to clear the hurdle.

3. TEASE THE AUDIENCE.

No matter how brief the speech, the audience's attention can lag. That's when you have to snap them back to your side, usually with a rhetorical device that makes them pay rapt attention again.

In this toast, the rhetorical device is a teaser ("But I'll come to that in a minute."). It piques the audience's interest, heightens anticipation, and perhaps creates a little anxiety (which isn't always bad). The audience becomes more alert waiting for the mystery to be resolved.

Of course, at some point you have to return to the point you raised and fill in the blanks. Audiences will hang on every word, but they don't like to be left hanging forever.

4. GET SERIOUS.

A speech cannot be all charm and fluff. At some point, you have to strike a serious note. It doesn't have to be overbearing or sentimental.

In this toast, the best man gets serious by talking about the commitment involved in a marriage. He doesn't preach. He merely salutes the bridal couple for making a commitment that has eluded him. It's a touching counterpoint to all the fluff that has come before. But you need both seriousness and fluff to make each other stand out clearly.

177

5. WRAP IT UP QUICKLY.

There's nothing more charming (or more appreciated by an audience) than ending a speech *before* everyone wants you to do so. In this toast, where the defined purpose is to salute the couple, the best man does his job at the end with one swift salutatory sentence.

I suspect the purpose of any other type of speech could be achieved with equal brevity and swiftness. If you're taking a long time to wrap things up, your audience will not be charmed.

CHAPTER 9

Hunting for a Job

WHAT'S THE RÉSUMÉ IN YOUR MIND?

A friend and I were discussing the hundreds of résumés that
cross our desks each year. I remarked how frustrating it was for
me to see all these excellent résumés and know that there
weren't any openings at our company for these young people.
I worried that our company was letting a whole generation of
talented people go elsewhere or, worse, to our competition.

My friend stunned me with his view of the situation.

"I don't see it that way at all," he said. "The only frustrating thing about all these résumés is their incredible *same-
ness*! All the candidates have good grades, perfect references,
interesting extracurricular activities, MBAs from top schools,
even some on-the-job experience. Just once I'd like to see a résumé that told me something about that person's character,

about who he or she really is. Just once I'd like to see the résumé that's in their mind, not the one on paper."

I see his point. There can be a tremendous disparity between the achievements people hold dearest in their mind and the achievements they actually put down in writing.

I see this in my case. I haven't had to write a résumé in thirty-five years, but I approve the biographical material that is sent out about me and our company. The data is almost like a résumé: played golf in college; trained as a lawyer; met Arnold Palmer; created sports marketing industry; built an international company with thirteen hundred employees in forty-nine offices in twenty-two countries . . .

Those are the achievements on paper.

But if I was being totally candid, I might admit to being prouder of an entirely different set of accomplishments.

Perhaps it's the fact that I managed Palmer, Player, and Nicklaus for ten years when it was such an obvious conflict and what that says about my people skills.

Perhaps it's the fact that our senior executives have been with the company an average of eighteen years and what that says about their loyalty to me and vice versa.

Perhaps it's my contribution to the game of golf by writing my *Golf Annual* for the last twenty-seven years or by creating the Sony Ranking.

Perhaps it's a favor I did twelve years ago for a friend's son and how that gave him a start in business.

All of these items could give a stranger a much richer insight into my character. And yet none of these items would normally go into a résumé—because it's hard to articulate their significance and pointing them out comes very close to boasting.

180

It's no different for any other job candidate.

Let's say that you saved your best friend from drowning or that for eighty-six Sundays in a row you have helped run a soup kitchen for homeless people simply because you felt you needed to do that. Those are character traits that are quite extraordinary, but they are not something that you can inject very easily into the standard-issue résumé.

And yet, if I were a prospective employer, those are precisely the qualities that I would like to know about an individual and that might help me choose between seemingly equal prospects.

One reason you don't see this sort of candor on résumés, I imagine, is that a lot of job candidates don't think that running a soup kitchen would impress the IBMs and General Electrics of this world when they're recruiting. Perhaps they believe that the IBM and GE recruiters would rather see that they ran the student government in college or served as chairman of the Homecoming committee.

Another problem, of course, is that, even if you think they are important, highlighting these achievements on paper is virtually impossible. "Saved best friend from drowning" somehow looks out of place on the same page with your 3.8 grade point average. And writing down that you run a soup kitchen can backfire on you. It can make you appear a little too calculating and self-congratulatory, as if you are doing that good deed, in part, so it looks good on a résumé.

It's not much easier to inject these achievements into an oral interview—even when the interviewer looks up from your résumé and says, "Okay, tell me what you're really like."

So how do prospective employees expose their proudest accomplishments to prospective employers?

181

The first step is to be subtle about it but not shy. Prospects should be smart enough to realize that, like my friend above, employers are hungering for this sort of information.

The second step is to realize that these qualities are usually best heard not directly from you but from other people. That's what references are for. If I wanted an employer to know I saved my best friend from drowning, I'd list that friend as a reference (and identify him simply as "friend"). If I wanted an employer to know of my voluntarism at the soup kitchen, I'd list the kitchen's director as a reference (and identify him simply as "soup kitchen director"). I guarantee those sorts of references will provoke some curiosity from your interviewer—certainly more so than listing three bosses or three professors.

There's nothing sly or manipulative about this, not if it helps worthy people shine a light on their true achievements and makes it easier for employers to get a better reading of a candidate's character.

IT'S THE COVER LETTER, NOT THE RÉSUMÉ, THAT REVEALS YOU

I'm always a little amazed by the extremes that people take in preparing their résumé. They spend hours, perhaps days, working and reworking every line describing their professional experience. Then they show the résumé to friends, inviting suggestions which inevitably induce another round of corrections. Then they choose a typeface that "expresses" their personality. Some people even spend hours deciding on the color, weight, and texture of the paper the résumé is printed on.

Don't get me wrong. I'm not knocking people who take the time to produce a smart résumé that accentuates their virtues. But all that effort seems a little misguided. I think people greatly overestimate the scrutiny their résumés receive out in the marketplace. Perhaps they think that their future employer can read between the lines of their résumé and somehow plumb the essence of their soul or find clues that prove their unworthiness as a candidate.

The real story is much more mundane.

For most people at most companies, reviewing résumés is a straightforward process that takes seconds rather than minutes or hours. They match the candidate's experience with the job. If they are looking for a sales manager, they toss out any résumé that doesn't contain sales experience. In that context, there really are no mysteries and no hidden clues in a résumé.

I know I don't spend too much time trying to read between the lines of a résumé. If I have questions, I can get a straight answer in our interview.

I suppose if I were more alert or devoted more time to the matter I could detect some clues in a résumé. After all, some red flags flap in front of your face. But they may also lead to flawed conclusions. If a candidate has changed jobs every ten months for the last four years, that may indicate a jumpiness and instability you might not want at your company. But then again, the candidate may have a valid reason for each move, anything from layoffs to spouse relocation. You'll never know unless you meet the candidate face to face. If you misread that red flag, you may miss out on a great employee.

In my experience, the cover letter that accompanies the résumé is a far more revealing document and a better indicator of a candidate's worthiness. Résumés, by definition, are generic. They adhere to a rigid format and, after so much massaging and polishing, they totally lack any personality. They could belong to anyone.

Cover letters, on the other hand, require some ingenuity. That's where the standout candidates actually stand out.

A well-written cover letter tells me something about the candidate's ability to articulate his or her thoughts. (A cover letter written in the dry, artificial tones of memospeak tells me something too, although it's hardly positive.)

A cover letter that misspells my name tells me something about the candidate's precision or lack thereof.

A cover letter that contains a clever idea is a sign of bold thinking—and not the sort of thing normally gleaned from a résumé.

Almost anything is a clue. I received an impressive résumé the other day, but what tipped the scales for the candidate was her cover letter and the fact that she took the time to type in the correct French accents on the word "résumé." A small sign perhaps, but just the sort of perfectionism that was needed in one of our divisions. I passed her name on to an executive in need of an assistant. Not surprisingly, she was as impressive in person as in writing—and got the job.

THREE WAYS TO RUIN A
JOB INTERVIEW

When you consider all the shelf space in stores devoted to books on job hunting, preparing the perfect résumé, and making a great impression on interviews, you'd think everyone would land a job his or her first time out. The basic rules—e.g., arrive on time, shake hands firmly, don't sit down until invited to do so (it shows good manners), be self-confident but don't brag about yourself, don't overstay your welcome—are simple and easy to follow.

But even within these forgiving parameters I've noticed a lot of young candidates are finding new ways to ruin their chances in job interviews. Here are three errors interviewees seem to be repeating at our company:

1. DON'T SEND A THANK-YOU NOTE.

This is something that all the job-hunting and etiquette books advise. It's not only polite, but it's another chance to get your name in front of your prospective boss. It's also another chance to demonstrate that you really want the job. You can't overestimate the power of eagerness. All things being equal, it will tip the scales in your favor.

More important, a thank-you note is an opportunity to do something special. One of our executives was interviewing prospective assistants with strong organizational skills. One candidate joked that even her sock drawer was perfectly organized. When she sent her thank-you note, she included a Polaroid snapshot of her sock drawer. Not a big deal, but it showed charm and ingenuity—and landed her the job. But it wouldn't have happened without the note.

2. Argue with the interviewer.

I realize that interviewers have all sorts of trick questions and brainteasers to provoke candidates, test their ingenuity, or see how they handle stress. I also appreciate that many interviewers are looking for strong-minded candidates who are not afraid to voice their opinions. But I don't know any interviewers who are impressed with a candidate who argues with them on the first meeting.

This trap is easier to fall into than you might imagine. For example, one of our executives mentioned a pet project during an interview. The young interviewee, eager to demonstrate the breadth of his knowledge, launched into an unsolicited critique of the concept and why it wouldn't work. Our executive gave the young man a chance to remove his foot from his mouth by saying some nice things about the project, but the young man persisted in arguing his case. That sort of aggression might work once you're inside the company but not when you're knocking on the door.

Remember, you're selling yourself in an interview. Even the most naive salespeople know not to argue with their customers. So should you.

3. Look for a promotion.

By far the worst thing you can do in an interview is apply for one job but let it be known that you're really interested in the spot immediately above it. It's not that interviewers are put off by your ambition. Every company is looking for bright, ambitious people.

But when people interview candidates, they usually have a specific job in mind that they urgently need to fill. And they have a reasonable expectation that the winning candidate will stay in that job for at least a year. It's pure self-interest. No boss wants to go through the hiring process every two or three months.

So keep your ambitions to yourself. Before you can launch yourself to bigger and better things, you have to get your foot in the door. You won't do that by seeking a promotion before you've even started.

LETTERS I'LL IGNORE

When it comes to writing business letters, I heed the Law of Diminishing Returns: The longer the letter, the less likely it will be answered. I know this is true because of all the long letters that I ignore.

You'd think that the people besieging busy executives with long letters, some with very good proposals, would learn this by now. But they don't.

Perhaps they think a long letter will impress the reader (it won't). Or that a good idea needs to be explained in five pages (if it's really good, ten words will do). Or that length will convince the reader they have every angle covered (usually the opposite is the case).

Length isn't the only reason letters go ignored. Here are three more:

1. Asking the Reader to Do Too Much

People who write letters that require the recipient to do too much have a good chance of getting ignored.

A business acquaintance in London once wrote to me about his thirteen-year-old son who wanted to get into the sports business. The father was seeking my advice but in such a way that he was literally asking me for a four-page letter mapping out his son's future. That's too much work (not to mention that it's really his responsibility). I ended up writing a one-page letter, but that sort of request is very close to what I'll ignore.

Make your requests simple ones. This can be nothing more than "Think about it" or "Read this and call me to discuss it." If you give your readers easy things to do, they're more likely to do it.

2. No Return Address on the Letterhead

Not everyone, I've discovered, writes on corporate letterhead. They often write on personal stationery, with only their name engraved on the sheet and the return address on the envelope. Unfortunately, envelopes have a way of getting lost or tossed out, leaving the reader with a name, an interesting proposal, and no way to pursue it.

If your stationery doesn't have a return address (and it should), tell people how to contact you in the body of the letter.

3. ORGANIZED WITH TOO MUCH LOGIC, NOT ENOUGH CARE

Many people are too logical. They organize their letters as if they were step-by-step proofs, saving the punch line for last. This may work in mathematics, but there's no guarantee it will grab or hold an executive's interests.

I received a letter the other day that was a model of careful organization. The young man looking for a job began: "I have now decided that you truly are as busy as you claim to be."

To me, that opening was too intriguing to ignore. And so I continued reading for two pages about his efforts to contact me, his family background, and his career plans. He closed by warning me, "I will try your office every day to try and meet with you."

I may not have a job for that young man, but he certainly commands my attention.

CHAPTER 10

Advanced Techniques

THE MESSENGER CHANGES THE
MESSAGE'S MEANING

I once gave a speech in Stockholm on behalf of the Swedish
Post Office on the subject of how to be more street-smart with
written communication. I talked about how well-crafted letters and memos can accomplish everything from recording
what was said in a meeting to suggesting (by their appearance, precision, and timeliness) how you conduct yourself in
other areas of business. But the biggest response from the
Swedish audience came when I told them the following story
about John DeLorean.

Long before his well-documented rise and fall as an automobile entrepreneur in the early 1980s, John DeLorean was
a fast-rising star at General Motors. Not long after he was

promoted to run GM's Pontiac division, DeLorean paid a visit to one of his regional offices. The regional manager, eager to impress the new chief, met DeLorean at the airport and took him to his hotel. As he entered his suite, DeLorean was greeted by an enormous basket of fruit containing more apples, oranges, peaches, and pears than he could eat in a year. Amused by this slight overkill, DeLorean turned to his aide and joked, "What, no bananas?"

Apparently, the aide took DeLorean's comment seriously—because the message swept through the Pontiac hierarchy that John DeLorean loved bananas. For years thereafter, wherever he went, he would see bananas. He would go into a divisional meeting in Europe and there at his place at the table was a bowl of bananas. A car would be dispatched to pick him up at the airport and in the backseat he would find bananas.

"I was only kidding," DeLorean told me. "I don't particularly like bananas."

But that's what happens to opinions expressed by high-ranking people. The people to whom these comments are directed tend to take them very seriously, often attaching more weight to them than intended. These same people also tend to act on the comment—the greater the authority, the quicker they act—which can produce some comical or disastrous results.

Someone once told me about John Hay Whitney, the wealthy venture capitalist and former U.S. ambassador to Great Britain, who, in the 1930s, was an active polo player. He was walking his estate in Manhasset, New York, one day with his groundskeeper and, assessing several acres of rolling hills and trees, wondered out loud how a polo field would look on this acreage.

The next day he sailed off to Europe for six months. On his return he was shocked to find that the groundskeeper had cleared and leveled those acres to build Mr. Whitney a polo field—at a cost of $300,000.

The larger point I am trying to make is that people tend to overreact to verbal comments made by their superiors. That principle is compounded when those same comments are put down in writing.

The more success you achieve, the higher you climb in an organization, the more authority you are perceived as having, the more important it is to realize this. Rank has a big impact on how a memo or letter is interpreted. People don't read the opinions of a junior executive the same way they would read the same opinions from the CEO.

If the chairman of Volvo one day concludes that his company should be making more light blue Volvos and expresses that in a memo to his director of manufacturing, chances are that message will not be dismissed lightly—because of the rank of the messenger. It will almost be treated as an edict.

Yet if that same memo were written by the manufacturing director's peer—say, the marketing director—the reaction would be more muted. The two executives might get together to discuss the subject or they might exchange a series of memos (in what may be the start of a "memo war").

If that memo to the manufacturing director were written by a junior staff person at Volvo, someone with no authority who just happened to like light blue Volvos, I suspect the director would read it, toss it out, and never think about it again.

One message. Three messengers. Three different ranks. Three radically different reactions.

Remember this the next time you put your opinions down in writing. The higher you rise in business the more careful you have to be. The strong or intemperate opinions you could get away with in your youth may not be appropriate now that people really pay attention to you.

All of us change as messengers during a career. Our messages should change too.

How to Bury the Lead (or Why the Third Item People Bring Up Is the One That Really Matters to Them)

One of the biggest sins in journalism is called "burying the lead"—when a writer devotes the first four or five paragraphs of the story to leisurely, unfocused prose rather than telling the reader what the story is about. Of course, there are sometimes valid artistic reasons for clearing your throat at the beginning of a story—to describe the setting or establish a point of view— but as a general rule, busy readers want instant gratification. If you want to hold their attention in any written communication, get to the point as soon as possible.

The opposite is true in oral communications. Refreshing as it may be to deal with someone who gets straight to the point in every conversation, in my experience most people can't handle such a blunt approach. They need to be massaged with small talk. They want you to "bury the lead."

Everyone appreciates this. The wife of one of my favorite golf clients once told me, "Everyone who calls us wants something from my husband. But each conversation is the same: The third thing they say is what they're really after. It's a predictable pattern. First, they ask about me and the children. Second, they mention something in the news or the sports pages, like, 'Did you see what so and so did in Texas?' Finally, they get to the point, which is what they wanted all along."

It's hard to argue with this. It's only human nature to start off with one or two nonconfrontational items before plunging into more serious issues. All of us bury our leads. In fact, the tactic is so common that it often loses its meaning. Like the client's wife above, we know when we're being manipulated or verbally stroked. We wait for the other shoe to fall.

I seriously question how effective burying the lead can be when it is so transparent. To have any value, it must be done artfully.

Perhaps the most rudimentary form of burying the lead occurs when we offer something to the other side before we ask them for something. For example, quite often the small talk with business associates centers on your respective spouses and children. If, in the natural course of such seemingly casual conversation, you can find a way to offer to do something nice for that person's family—e.g., help their son or daughter find a summer job—that gesture, whether it is accepted or not, will increase the chances that the third item on your agenda, the item you really want, will be more favorably received.

I'm amazed how often people fail to see this tactic being employed on them. It happens to me. I still end some phone calls chastising myself for being too generous or accommodating with the other party. "Why did I commit to doing that?" I ask myself. "Why did I give away more than I wanted?" Invariably, when I replay the conversation in my mind, I find that early in the dialogue the other party has softened me up by offering me something first.

As I say, this is a rudimentary tactic. But it works.

I learned to bury the lead after several years of representing Arnold Palmer. In those days, I traveled a lot with Arnold. However, on the occasions when I stayed home in Cleveland to attend to Arnold's business while he was on the road playing golf, a strange dynamic developed between us. I could be working fifteen-hour days for Arnold in Cleveland, but in Arnold's mind I was loafing while he was out there working. As a result, when Arnold returned home for some much-needed rest, it could be very difficult to persuade him to commit his time and energy to some of the projects I wanted him to do.

So I developed a strategy where I would front-load our meetings with items that I didn't care if he rejected and bury the item I really needed him to approve.

I'd start off with a minor request from one of his sponsors for three hours of photography sometime that week. Not surprisingly, Arnold would say no, citing the perfectly valid reason that he wanted to rest.

I'd follow this with a request from a Pittsburgh newspaper to come out to the house to profile Arnold and his wife. Again, Arnold would say no.

After a few more of these summary rejections, I could see Arnold feeling a little guilty about shooting down my requests. A look of sympathy would be etched on his face.

That's when I would present him with the request that really mattered.

Before you can artfully bury the lead, of course, you have to determine precisely what it is. This is not as easy as it sounds. There are a lot of forces in a business dialogue that can make you lose your way. But the essential dynamic—i.e., the third thing is what they're really after—prevails in even the most convoluted discussions.

I once had a one-hour meeting with the chairman of a large communications company. The meeting had taken months to arrange and I had mentioned it to at least a dozen people in our company. They, in turn, bombarded me with memos outlining ideas I should be pitching to the chairman—everything from sponsoring a volleyball league to Joe Montana videos. In other words, I had an enormous list of leads to choose and bury.

I suppose I could have cherry-picked the most clever or expensive ideas from these memos and presented them in such a way that the chairman would be impressed by one or two.

But my main agenda, I decided, was to get to know the chairman and help him get to know me. I'd met him twice before, but always informally in groups, never alone. In the sixty minutes I had with him, he and I spent at least thirty minutes talking about our careers and our respective golf games. I managed to slip in two key points—that our company was a big customer of his company's services and that we were international, which dovetailed nicely with his growing interest in international markets.

As we talked it became obvious to me that this chairman was operating at such a lofty and detached level in his organization that he would have absolutely no hands-on role

197

in anything that I presented to him. He would have no impact on deciding which golfer gets hired for a customer entertainment program in Georgia or whether the western region wants to sponsor six figure-skating events. Getting to know each other was a worthy goal, but for getting decisions made at his company, it appeared to be irrelevant.

But I was encouraged by how friendly he was, so I decided to share my dilemma with him. Rather than be coy or subtle, I unburied my lead and told him, "The people in our company who know about this meeting have deluged me with memos about everything we've done, are doing, and should be doing with your company and with whom we are doing them. I'm not going to waste your time with all that in this meeting. But I've distilled all these memos into five ideas which I can describe in one or two sentences. If you're interested in any of them, I will respond by writing to you in a concise manner that is responsive to all the questions you will have."

I then went through the five ideas, all of which intrigued him. Then I asked him about the five people in his company to whom we had already presented these ideas—to see how he would rate them or even if he knew them. He knew two out of the five and had a high opinion of both.

I'm not positive we'll make a sale, but now that I know what ideas interest the chairman and which of his executives will give us a fair hearing, I'm extremely confident about our chances. I doubt if I would have learned any of this if I hadn't spent the first half of our meeting on "small talk" and the second half forthrightly telling him exactly what I wanted.

NO MATTER HOW POWERFUL YOUR WRITING, ONE VISIT IS STILL WORTH A THOUSAND LETTERS

I'm a lawyer by training, and like most lawyers, I have an inordinate respect for the power of the written word. That respect was initially drilled into me at Yale Law School in the mid-1950s. Spend three years studying the written opinions of this country's greatest legal minds (as any law student must do) and you, too, will renew your appreciation of powerful, persuasive writing.

I suppose that's one reason lawyers are so quick to send aggressive, threatening letters to the other side when their clients are embroiled in a potential legal dispute. They actually believe the written word can enlighten or intimidate the other party and turn that party around to their point of view.

I know I believed this in my early years. But I've gradually come to the conclusion that trying to persuade people in writing, particularly on a legal issue, is one of the most time-inefficient and counterproductive methods at your disposal.

I learned this back in the 1970s when one of our athlete clients agreed to become the spokesperson for a large European leisure company, whose managing director happened to be the athlete's longtime friend. Because of this friendship, even though the terms of the deal were complicated, the athlete went to work for the company based on a verbal commitment from the managing director while we worked out the fine points of a formal contract.

The athlete was clear about the terms. For committing to six days of promotional work a year, he would be paid a spe-

199

cific fee and also receive a forty-five-foot boat, which the company manufactured.

The relationship worked out very well. In fact, the conglomerate underestimated the number of days they needed from our client, so that within three months, and before we had a chance to get a signed agreement, they had already used up the athlete's six days. We were delighted at the prospect of negotiating new terms.

Unfortunately, we had not counted on the company changing ownership and the managing director taking a new job at another company. His replacement, eager to put his stamp on the company in a decisive and highly visible way, decided to cancel the arrangement with our client. The new managing director instructed his business affairs people to pay our client's fee but not to give him the boat.

Our client wrote a very testy letter to the new managing director about this situation, contending that he had worked for and was entitled to the boat.

Thus began an amazing chain of letters.

The new managing director fired off an equally testy letter, arguing that there was no formal agreement and that, if anything, our client's gripe was with the previous owners of the company. The athlete, with the help of a lawyer, wrote several letters pointing out that he had fulfilled his part of the arrangement and was "abandoned" when the company changed hands. He didn't dispute the company's right to cancel the deal, but it was clear that the boat had become a matter of principle to him.

This went on for nearly eighteen months, at which point I got a look at the entire file. What surprised me most about the correspondence was the tone of the athlete's letters. This athlete was one of the most charming and reasonable gentlemen I had ever met (that was one reason the company hired him in the first place). But the person I met in the correspondence (no doubt written by lawyers) was petulant, charmless, and not very attractive. It was clear that each letter was harming rather than helping his cause and we were heading toward expensive litigation, which the other side could afford more easily than could our client.

I had a hunch that if the managing director met our client the outcome would be different. A meeting was arranged and, although I wasn't present, I understand our client was brilliant. He immediately picked up that the issue had become more personal than legal when the managing director opened the meeting by quoting some of the more stinging lines from his first letter.

The athlete was deferential, self-effacing, and sensitive to the managing director's position. He pointed out, however, that everyone occasionally has a matter of principle in their life that is really important to them. It wasn't the money or the boat that mattered but rather his sense of fair play. He felt that he wasn't being treated fairly.

The following day we received a letter from the managing director confirming that the agreement would be honored (boat included) and inquiring about terms for a multiyear agreement with our client.

As I say, one visit is usually more valuable than a thousand letters.

THE "WHO WE ARE" MEMO

When *Washington Post* reporters Bob Woodward and Carl Bernstein began their investigation of the Watergate break-in in 1972—which eventually forced Richard Nixon's resignation and made them media superstars—the most valuable piece of information they had was the White House telephone directory.

This was the document that not only gave them names and numbers, but told them who was working for whom at the White House, who they could call to confirm or deny a rumor, and who was close to the President and his cabinet officers.

I often wish I had a telephone directory for each company I called on—because it would be invaluable to know who was working for whom, who could give me straight answers to my questions, and who could get me through to a decisionmaker. But, of course, that's the information you can rarely get.

To an outsider, most corporate bureaucracies are, by design, a mystery. (They are often a mystery to insiders as well, but that's another story.) Companies don't ordinarily broadcast to the world how they are structured or who their key personnel are and what they are working on. Nor should they.

I don't have a problem with bureaucracies that are secretive or mysterious—even though it makes our salespeople's jobs more difficult.

But I've come to realize that there is one instance when this sort of secrecy can be counterproductive—when you apply it to companies you are already doing business with.

This was brought home to me a few years ago when I entered into an agreement with Careertrack, a Colorado-based business seminar company, to produce and market a seminar series based on my book, *What They Don't Teach You at Harvard Business School.*

How Careertrack planned to do this, frankly, was a mystery to me. I knew the process of developing a seminar, finding the appropriate seminar leaders, designing brochures, marketing the program, and getting people to attend would be complicated.

But Careertrack opened my eyes—with a piece of correspondence that is all too often missing at the start of promising relationships. I call this the "Who We Are" memo.

A few weeks after we signed the agreement, the company sent us a five-page letter. In it, they outlined an eleven-step program on preparing a production schedule, designing brochures, selecting seminar cities, etc. They spelled out exactly how they would be developing the program and what they would need from me each step of the way.

But what was unique about the letter was that at the end of each step, highlighted in bold letters, was the name and telephone number of an employee—the "champion" at Careertrack who would get that task done.

In effect, they were giving us a phone directory to their company. Only they went one better. They not only were telling us "Who We Are" but also "How We Work."

This was one of the more refreshing and reassuring letters I've received. It reminded me of several relationships we have had over the years which started out on a solid footing and then fell apart because of miscommunication—because either we weren't clearly told how the other side operated or we didn't tell them the same thing about us.

It reminded me that, once you've come to an agreement, a "Who We Are" memo lifting the veil of mystery about your company is perhaps more valuable for the long-term health of a relationship than a contract.

For years I've made it a point at the end of a meeting, in which both sides have agreed on a course of action, to establish clear lines of communications—who would be talking to whom about what. Now I put that down in writing.

THE INDIRECT ROUTE OFTEN LEADS TO DIRECT RESULTS

I am by nature a frontal person. A straight line has always been the best and easiest way for me to get things done. If I want to close a sale, I ask for the order. If I don't know something, I admit it. If I need help, I ask for it. If I'm troubled by something, I let someone know about it. I recommend this approach to everyone.

But I recognize that there are occasions in life when a straight line is not the appropriate course for getting from Point A to Point B. Sometimes a detour to Points C, G, and L can save you a lot of time and grief.

Here are four indirect approaches that can help you solve some all-too-common situations.

1. Ask provocative questions.

Sometimes when you want someone to do something for you, the worst thing you can do is order them to do it.

For example, it may be very important to me that our senior executives get a better handle on how effective their division meetings are and what their people think of those meetings. But for me to insist that they formally evaluate each meeting, to the point where I suggest that they hand out questionnaires to the attendees and actually tell them what to ask in the questionnaires, may be perceived as meddling in their affairs. They may misinterpret the suggestion as an accusation that they are running disorganized meetings.

For some reason, people respond more favorably to a provocative question than to a reasonable demand. Thus, instead of insisting that executives tighten up their meetings, I might ask each executive privately, "When you had that meeting last month, what did all the employees say when you asked what you could do to improve the meeting?" I know fully well that the executive hasn't done this sort of evaluation. But he doesn't know I know that. And if he's as good as I think he is, next time he will.

2. Use a proxy to get the truth.

Sometimes you need information from people but because of your position in the company, you suspect that you won't get a sincere answer. That's when you need a third party to get to the truth.

Most of us already do this socially. As teenagers, before we ask a boy or girl out on a date, we might first have a mutual friend find out how the object of our attention feels about us.

It's a little more complicated in business. For example, once you reach a certain level of authority at your company, you should recognize that your subordinates may be editing a lot of the information they give you. They prefer to give you good news rather than bad news, even though it's far more important that you get the bad news (so you can correct it). For that reason alone you might need to use a trusted and disinterested proxy to dig up the truth.

A few years ago, a CEO I know had a hunch that his company's computer operations were underperforming and hurting the company. So he called a formal meeting with his computer wizards and invited them to speak freely, without reprisal, about what was wrong with the system. The meeting went nowhere, because none of the wizards was willing to admit to being less than wizardly in front of the CEO. A task force to study the situation was equally futile, since everyone on the task force knew each other and knew that their report would be read by the CEO.

Finally, the CEO transferred a young executive from the London office to work in the computer department. This "mole" didn't have an important title and he wasn't a computer expert. But he was good at understanding organizational behavior and getting people to talk to him. Within a month, he identified the problems, reported them to the CEO, and no one was the wiser.

3. USE A THIRD PARTY AS YOUR ADVOCATE.

Sometimes you may want something to happen but you are not in the best position to advocate such a course of action. It may be misinterpreted or confuse the situation.

For example, if I want a particular executive in our organization to relocate to Berlin, it may be counterproductive for me to suggest that. The executive may think I'm making an onerous demand or being cavalier with his career. He may not appreciate that this is a major step up the ladder, no matter how much I reassure him.

I might achieve the desired result if I have a third party float the idea first. I would have one of this executive's peers discuss the move. They might say, "If I weren't married or the kids weren't starting school, I'd jump at this opportunity." That statement may change his perception. If he hears this often enough from his peers, the executive may eventually realize that going to Berlin is a real plum rather than just a job I need to fill.

4. SUGGEST THE IMPOSSIBLE.

The easiest way for someone to get me to do something is to suggest that I'm incapable of doing it.

If someone said to me, "Gee, Mark, it's too bad you're too busy to come talk to my sales group . . ." I might respond to that. That person has given me a challenge and, since I'm competitive by nature, I might go out of my way to confound the limitations he has imposed on me.

People who are competitive like to be confronted with what other people think are impossible mountains to climb so

207

they can demonstrate how easy it is for them to climb those mountains.

A few years ago a friend said to me, "I would give anything to meet the chairman of XYZ Corp. because I have an idea that would really be good for them. But it's impossible for me to do that." I asked him to share the idea with me and told him I might be able to do something about it.

It took me two weeks and perhaps more phone calls and favors than it was worth, but I arranged a meeting with the chairman for this fellow. To this day, I'm not sure if he floated that suggestion innocently or was manipulating me. But he tempted me with an impossible assignment and, predictably, I accepted the challenge.

THE HIGH ART OF HANDLING THE PRESS

A chief executive was complaining to me once about how his company was always getting skewered in the press. "If we're not misquoted," he said, "then the facts are distorted and the tone is very negative."

I asked him who was responsible for his press relations.

He said, "Oh no. We have a policy of never talking to the press." Which, I guess, explains everything.

It would be nice to write off this CEO as a Neanderthal in the ways of modern media, with no one to blame but himself. But I know plenty of smart executives who actively court journalists, hire publicists, and maintain a clipping service to track every mention of their name—and they fare no better in the press.

The point is, the press doesn't like you to be too familiar or too remote. Somewhere in between is a media policy that works. Here's how to get there.

1. DON'T ARGUE WITH THE PRESS.

It raises the dialogue to fever pitch, and the quotes always come out more hostile and more combative than you intended.

Members of the press are like any other profession. Some are honorable and bright. Some are dishonorable and dim. But they have a unique weapon unknown to other professions. They always have the last word. And you can't argue with that.

2. GIVE THEM AS MUCH (OR MORE) TIME THAN THEY NEED.

You can't blame reporters for getting the facts wrong or disliking you if you only give them one hour when they ask for three.

3. KEEP YOUR SECRETS FOR AS LONG AS YOU CAN.

I've never been a great fan of press attention, especially the kind initiated by publicists. I find that any business strategy works better the longer you keep the competition unaware of it.

If you're big enough within your industry, your secretiveness can actually damage your competitors—or at least distract them. IBM, for example, never comments on any new product in development. As a result, a cottage industry of experts has arisen to read the meaning of IBM's "refusal to comment." The experts are rarely right, and even if they were, I certainly wouldn't base my company's future on them.

4. IF YOU MUST TALK, HAVE A STRATEGY.

Even though we never solicit publicity, we still have gotten some nice attention. In the sports business, if you do your job well, people will want to write about it.

If you must blow your own horn, at least have a strategy for doing so.

In the mid-1970s, when it seemed that I was the only person who knew the scope and significance of our company, *Sports Illustrated* approached us about an article. I decided to go overboard in cooperating with them, to insure that they position us accurately as the dominant company in our field. That's when they called me "the most powerful man in sports."

At the time, the article was an eye-opener to many people in and out of our industry. People who should have known better would come up to me and say, "We had no idea you were doing all these things." This wasn't surprising. We're a private company. Until that article appeared, there was no way people could have known.

5. USE THE MEDIA'S HUNGER AND SHORT MEMORY.

The media is a hungry beast. It constantly needs fresh material. It also has a very short memory. Couple that enormous appetite for stories with a short attention span, and you have an interesting mix that can work to your advantage.

For example, in the late 1980s, it again seemed to me that I was the only person aware that our company had made an exponential leap in the scope of its activities. We had quintupled in size to more than a thousand employees since that eye-opening *Sports Illustrated* article. So once again we cooperated fully when *Sports Illustrated* wanted to do an exposé about us. We let the magazine's reporters rummage through our business for nine months. Once again, the resulting article in 1990 opened a lot of people's eyes about us and positioned us for the rest of the decade. We liked it so much, we bought five thousand reprints to hand out on sales calls. As for *Sports Illustrated*, they not only called me "the most powerful man in sports" again, they used it as the story's title.

6. HAVE A STRATEGY FOR SILENCE, TOO.

Of course, there are times to keep quiet about how well you're doing. If we represent one hundred basketball players, we will lose more from telling the world that secret than we can gain. We have the fleeting ego gratification of announcing "We're big!" But a shrewd competitor can sell against that fact. He can woo clients away by saying, "They handle so many basketball players, you're just another number." (This may be unfair to us but not unpersuasive to some clients.)

I'd rather let the world think we have thirty basketball clients even if we do have one hundred.

IT'S BETTER TO INVITE THAN WRITE

Over the years, I've seen every type of overture that college graduates can make when they want a job at our company. They send letters, pictures, résumés, and business proposals. They write to say how much they enjoy my books. They get mutual friends to write reference letters, send résumés, or deliver proposals. But the best strategy for getting through to me or any other executive has nothing to do with writing.

I was reminded of this in 1994 when I spoke at Northwestern's Kellogg School of Business in Chicago. I was there solely because of the persistence of an MBA student who had waged a one-man campaign since 1992 to lure me on campus. The young man must have called my office twenty times before I found a convenient date.

It never occurred to me that he might be interested in working for our company, but as the speech date approached he started bombarding my office with résumés and letters of reference. He had impressive credentials, but they weren't really necessary.

One of our executives took him aside and told him, "Look, you don't need all these letters. You've got the key decision-maker coming to you for a "meeting." You're going to be with him for half a day. You'll make a bigger impression in person than on paper. If the day goes well, you'll be miles ahead of all those other people who are still writing to our company."

I mention this not to generate more speeches on campus, but to point out how simple it is to meet decisionmakers on your turf. I don't know many executives who aren't flattered by an invitation to speak at a business school. In most cases, they'll show up if they can fit it into their schedule. For a smart job candidate that's a golden opportunity.

If you want to make a strong impression, don't write the CEO. Invite the CEO.

IS IT POSSIBLE TO COMMUNICATE TOO MUCH?

The short answer is no. You will never hear me telling people in our company that they're overcommunicating. If employees have a choice of writing a memo to a colleague or shrugging it off by telling themselves, "It's too minor to put down in writing!" or "I'll mention it the next time we see each other," I would always want employees to send the memo. You can never predict how vital the information may be to the person receiving that memo. When it comes to communicating, I want our people to err on the side of overkill.

Having said that, I think there is both intelligent and misguided overkill. Whether you're guilty of one or the other depends on how shrewd you are about the people receiving your message.

Here are five ways even the most ardent communicators go astray.

1. DON'T COMPLICATE THE PROCESS.

In a desire to make people more serious about communicating with one another, it's easy to fall into the trap of overcomplicating the process, of making the effort of communicating more difficult than the desired result.

Let's say one day I decide that I want to be better informed about all the sales presentations our executives are making. So I decree that everyone must write at least a five-page report on every sales call, documenting who was there, what was said, what promises were made, how the prospect reacted, and what will be done to follow up. The report cannot be less than five pages—because I want a complete report and I believe the exercise of writing such a lengthy document is worthwhile. It makes people take the meeting more seriously.

I can easily envision that some people might not take this edict well. I can also see how some people might end up spending more time writing their reports than making sales calls. Taken to its extreme, the report might even chill some salespeople's enthusiasm for sales calls. They might stop tracking down leads and having meetings to avoid writing the five-page report.

In communicating, good intentions can be ruined by a flawed process.

2. USE OVERKILL ONLY ON THOSE WHO NEED IT.

Some employees, like children, don't hear you the first time (or, for that matter, the second or third time). If you know that about a person, you can never be guilty of overcommunicating with them.

With such a person, I wouldn't hesitate to remind them five times or more, either personally or via a third party, to act on my request. The first time I might tell the executive directly, "Please call Tom Smith." Two days later, I might ask the executive's assistant, "Please remind your boss to call Tom Smith." Then I might ask a colleague to mention Tom Smith. And so on, until I get satisfaction. With some people this constant pin-pricking with the same message is not overkill. It's the only way to get through.

On the other hand, if someone tried that with me, I might get irritated. I don't need to be told more than once to do something.

3. USE OVERKILL ON THOSE WHO WANT IT.

Just as some people don't know they need overkill, others are aware of it and actually prefer it. This is often true with people who place as much value on the form of communication as its substance.

For example, if it's possible to explain a situation in a concise paragraph, I would always prefer a one-paragraph memo to anything longer. Yet I know people who would feel cheated or incompletely informed with anything less than a twenty-six-page document that gives them everything from the facts to the historical background to the supporting literature behind the background.

A short memo that would be doing me a favor would be an insult if not a sign of ignorance to some other boss.

4. BEWARE THE OPEN FORUM.

It's also possible to be too open and free in communicating. This is certainly true in meetings.

There's no perfect way to conduct a large meeting with employees. But if there's an option between having (a) a tightly controlled agenda where everyone has an allotted time to speak, and (b) an open forum where anyone can jump in anytime and there's no standing on rank or ceremony, the latter seems preferable. If nothing else, you'll know where people stand at meeting's end.

But there's a risk, and it's the same with any other form of overkill. Too much freedom can lead to chaos. If everyone in the room gets to voice an opinion, you're only a step or two away from totally losing any chance at achieving consensus. The process destroys the desired result.

5. BEWARE THE FAMILIAR VOICE.

I also think that frequency has an effect on the way people communicate with each other—and it's not always positive. It's quite possible to talk too much and too often to the same people.

I certainly see it in our company in the way people talk to me. There are some executives to whom I talk in person or on the phone maybe once a year. Their mode of communication with me is completely different from the mode of more familiar executives with whom I talk twice a day. It's the difference between, "Oh dear, the boss is on the phone!" and "Oh no, not the boss again!" That's not surprising. The more you talk to someone, the more relaxed the conversation.

But increased communication can eventually leave both parties with diminishing returns.

I remember a few years back having to call one of our executives on almost a daily basis about his activities. I think he enjoyed the increased attention from me, as if he had moved up a notch in some vague pecking order. But increased attention goes hand in hand with increased expectations. After a few conversations with the executive in which he spent twenty minutes describing the twenty-eight leads he was pursuing, I expected to hear some positive results from one or two of the leads. After a dozen conversations in which I heard about the same leads but never anything material or positive, the executive started to fall slightly in my estimation. I began to wonder how effective he was. Both of us would have benefited from talking less often to one another.

COLLECT DOVE'S LIBRARY OF
MARK H. McCORMACK
CLASSIC BUSINESS BOOKS AND AUDIOS

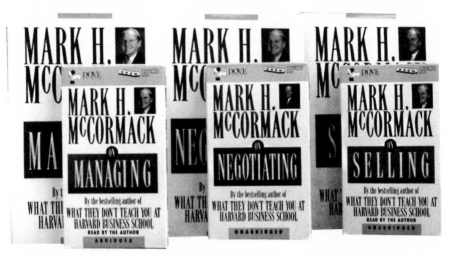

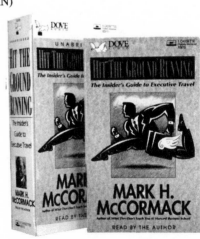

DOVE
ENTERTAINMENT

Available at bookstores everywhere or call 1-800-368-3007